Planting New Churches

D0726302

Planting New Churches

**George Carey
and others**

**Edited by Bob Hopkins
with Tim Anderson**

eagle
Guildford, Surrey

A catalogue record for this book is available from the British Library

ISBN 0 86347 043 2

Published by Eagle, an imprint of Inter Publishing Services (IPS) Ltd, Williams Building, Woodbridge Meadows, Guildford, Surrey GU1 1BH

Phototypeset by Intype, London
Printed in the UK by HarperCollins Manufacturing, Glasgow.

Front cover design: Martin Lore, DESK

Acknowledgements

There are many without whom this book could never have happened. Space only allows me to especially thank and name those most directly involved.

Of first importance is Tim Anderson who was responsible for helping me with a major part of the editorial task involved. He was the one who reviewed all the texts and tapes of the 34 speakers at our conference. From his publishing experience, he advised on the overall structure of this book as well as doing much tailoring and rewriting where necessary to bring the selected contributions into a coherent whole.

Secondly I want to thank Sandy Millar for making all the facilities of Holy Trinity Brompton available to us for the morning plenary sessions and the eight afternoon seminar venues – without any charge whatever. Rich Thorpe and the staff at Holy Trinity Brompton worked hard on all the practical arrangements, while from Holy Trinity Parr Mount, Geoff Firth and my wife Mary supervised all the correspondence and registrations, with the help of staff members and equipment from the YWAM base in St Helen's.

I also want to thank all those who spoke at the conference on 22nd May 1991 whether or not their material is included in this book. Everyone put a great deal of time and effort into preparing their material and there were many excellent presentations that are not included here. Selection had to be based principally on considerations of the overall structure of the book and material not already published elsewhere.

I do not want to forget the very significant part played by an army of unnamed intercessors who have prayed for our Anglican church planting network in general and for this annual conference in particular.

Last but not least, I want to thank our new Archbishop, the Most Revd Dr George Carey. As a diocesan bishop before his recent appointment he encouraged our Anglican church planting network over the previous three years. He was a keynote speaker at our 1988 conference and chairman in 1989. This support, together with that of Bishops Simon Barrington-Ward, Richard Hare and Colin Buchanan, played a key role in giving us hope to believe that church planting could be recognised as having a valid contribution to make to a contemporary mission strategy for the Church of England.

Bob Hopkins
St Helens

Contents

Foreword

The fact that many believe church planting to be the most effective form of evangelism is cited by more than one of the contributors to this book. This conviction makes this book particularly relevant to the Decade of Evangelism. It is also very appropriate for the decade, because many of the stories and principles shared here can apply to any church that wants to be more effective in evangelism and growth. In fact the book could have been subtitled *The Church as the Vehicle for Evangelism*.

The book has been compiled from the presentations at the fourth national day conference on Church Planting in the Church of England, held at Holy Trinity Brompton on 22nd May 1991. The recently enthroned Archbishop of Canterbury, Dr George Carey, gave the keynote address which forms Part One of the book. There were 33 other speakers, some in plenary sessions and some sharing in the afternoon seminars. Part Two is a selection of presentations by those speakers who told their stories of church planting experience from all sorts of different contexts and with contrasting approaches to their mission task. Part Three has contributions from some of the speakers who addressed more general issues and principles relating to church-planting evangelisation.

There were other excellent contributions that cannot be included here; a list of all sessions together with tapes available can be obtained from the address below. Similar material from the previous three national conferences is also available on request. These were held in May 1987, 1988 and 1989. There was no conference in 1990.

Over the five years since the first conference, the numbers attending have gone up by ten times, from about 70 to 700. This corresponds with the rapidly increasing trend of the statistics of numbers of Anglican plants, as shown in Figure 5 on page 173 presented by George Ling in Chapter 13. His graphs show a growing wave of church planting initiatives in the Church of England; and since his figures were put together we have heard of several other plants in the past two or three years.

Because this book focuses on church planting in the Church of England it will be of special interest to Anglicans. However, because of the particular difficulties that the Church of England presents to church planters (i.e. the parish and legal frameworks), there is a sense in which if it can happen here, it can certainly happen anywhere! Furthermore, many principles shown here are quite universal, applying to any church that wants to multiply and more effectively reach its neighbourhoods. This book will certainly contain plenty to help other churches/denominations within a parish structure. It will also be particularly relevant for the state churches of other European countries where church planting movements are just beginning.

Bob Hopkins
Holy Trinity Parish Office
YWAM Parr Mount School
Sorogold Street
St Helens WA9 1AX

Introduction

Bob Hopkins

This book is not intended to suggest that every church should have church planting as an aim; or that planting is the answer to every parish problem. But I believe that church planting is very significant. The energy released by church planting, which normally includes a focus on lay ministry and on evangelism, is likely to have important overflow effects on the life of the wider church.

The chapter by George Lings in this volume presents the statistics of Anglican church plants during the past 25 years. However, there are earlier forerunners, such as the Mission Hall movement and the Daughter Church movement. More recently, 1971 saw the first of six satellite congregations at Chester-le-Street; chapter 12 provides some reflections on that experience. Another modern pioneer was Ted Longman who in 1969, as curate at St Paul's Homerton in East London, broke the mould by starting a church plant on a Greater London Council estate, moving there and using his living room as a place to meet. Kingsmead comprised some 1,000 flats in sixteen blocks, within an area 300 yards square. In 1973 he wrote the story of what had occurred, and observed:

In recent years the church has failed to reach the working classes ... [the reason] is that every local

11

community, eg. council estate or block of flats, does not have its own local church ... the conclusion to all this is that we must have local churches which reflect the cultural pattern of their immediate area and which are easily accessible.[1]

In the last two decades, there has been a gathering wave of church planting activity. Some notable examples are described in the chapters that follow.

De-mythologising Church Planting

The case studies in this book, and many others like them, expose some false ideas and rumours about church planting. To emphasise this, I will mention some of the things that church planting is *not*:

It is *not just a 'Bible-belt suburbia' phenomenon*: almost half the Church of England plants are taking on the traditionally 'tough' areas, such as council estates, Urban Priority Areas and new towns.

It is *not a church within a church*: church planting at present is mainly, though not exclusively, within the evangelical tradition. That does not make it a church within a church. These periodic fires of renewed life in the different streams of the Church of England produce and maintain its comprehensiveness. The stories that follow include the plant to reach Asians by the Anglo-Catholic congregation in Hounslow and the re-opening of a closed church in a pair of linked parishes in Notting Hill whose traditions were both catholic and broad church. Other examples not documented include a rural Anglo-Catholic vicar planting a congregation into a village barn in the Ely Diocese and plans for an Anglo-Catholic plant into a block of flats in Tottenham.

It is *not comfortable triumphalism*: to read the chapters that follow is to see that church planting is not about comfortable, triumphant cliques but about a costly, sacrificial leaving of the nest, with no guarantee of success.

It is *not sectarian or eclectic*: although a few examples of recent church plants are due to the growth and multiplication of eclectic congregations, the vast majority are not. Even for those that are, the planting itself tends to break down their eclectic character. Most church plants are an expression of parish mission, the aim being to church the community and the neighbourhood.

It is *not controversial*: contrary to rumour and the impression conveyed by the press, only a tiny minority of church plants in the Church of England have been in any way controversial. The great majority have either been within their own parishes, or have crossed boundaries after negotiation and with full agreement of both bishops and receiving parishes. Of 35 plants known to have crossed boundaries, only three have caused any difficulty.

It is *not un-Anglican*: the suggestion that church plantings are superficial or just expressions of our obsession with new things is not reasonable. The church planting movement within the Church of England combines our appreciation of the historic roots of the church with the recognition of innovative moves of God. Together, these make the church powerful and appropriate for each new generation.

The Essence of Church Planting

If this is what church planting is *not*, we can ask what *is* the essence of church planting that lies behind all these initiatives? As I review this church planting explosion in the Church of England, it seems that there are three essential elements at the heart of the varied examples.

First, *it is part of mission*. Church planting is mission through the local church. Its prime motivation is to express the gospel in and for groups and neighbourhoods which are not being reached. As such, I am convinced that it has a key role in helping us move from maintenance to mission in the church.

Second, *the heart of church planting is church reproduction by multiplication*. This is like the spreading yeast cells to which Jesus likened the growth of the kingdom of God (Matt. 13:33). It means multiplying groups and multiplying all the leadership and ministry functions of the church. As with all ministry, it is a big challenge: a commitment to individual and corporate 'dying', like the grain of wheat which falls into the ground so that it may bear fruit. Sometimes, churches dwindle not for lack of workers, but for lack of challenges to which the workers can rise. Church planting changes that.

The third element is *incarnation*. The seed dies into the ground; and church planting means making the church body present in new places and for new people. Church planting is neighbourhood evangelisation. It represents an opportunity to turn the church inside out and help it to break out of any Christian ghetto it has become. Church planting means multiplying centres of worship and witness, to make the church more accessible and to multiply points of contact in the community. It also multiplies the models of church life available, in response to the mosaic of cultural, social and ethnic diversity in our nation. It could be one key for effective mission in Urban Priority Areas.

Seven Broad Types of Creative Planting

The variety and creativity of the case studies in this book will help to widen our understanding of how church planting principles can enliven the church's mission. I have developed seven broad classification types.

1. *Virgin plants* into a completely new housing area. This is the closest to classic church planting ideas from the foreign mission field. However, it can also include planting into an established area where a completely unreached ethnic or social group has been identified.

2. *Planting multiple parallel congregations*, usually into the same building. The church is not the building, so if a separate congregation is created, with its own leadership, patterns of worship, sub-group structures, ministry and outreach, then it has the essence of a church plant. In some cases the second congregation may have a very similar character to the first; but from Sheffield and Brixton Hill there are examples of very different congregations meeting at different times on a Sunday

3. *Planting vigour into decline*. There are now many examples of a planting team, or even a congregational transplant, being arranged to avoid closing a parish church or even to re-open one. When there is a struggling remnant, there needs to be sensitivity to those people, along with a willingness on their part to embrace the changes needed to bring growth.

4. *Transplanting strength or leadership*. This type of mission has been described by Martin Down and has similarities to type 3, but is significantly different.[2] In a town there may be eleven parishes, three strong and eight weaker. Plans to transplant a group from a strong church to a weaker one (where there is a desire

for help) could be a kind of plant. Again, if one of the weak churches were a village parish, with a vicar rarely available, offering a leader or lay-reader might be a key transplant strategy. This kind of church plant is not a take-over, but an injection to give a boost.

5. *Planting out into community structures*. This approach gets the church into organisations and existing structures in society, such as northern clubs, hospitals, or old people's homes.

6. *Planting out into neighbourhoods*. Again, this focuses the church away from a single-centre parish, and recognises discreet sub-divisions of community life. Ian Bunting has called this 'rediscovering the urban village', from his Chester-le-Street satellite experience. He draws from the Latin American 'Base Community' movement in modelling this type of plant. I describe it as churching the community; or neighbourhood evangelisation.

7. *Planting life into life*. It is not only where a church is struggling that it may call for help from another church. Examples are arising where one parish successfully develops a mission model for reaching a particular socio-cultural group. Then other parishes, with thriving congregations of their own, invite them to come and resource a new initiative to reach a similar group in their parish. This is a welcome change from protectionism and defensiveness, and recognises that most parishes with a full church of 300 attending on Sunday are still by no means adequately churched.

Is there a danger, with all these strategies for church planting and multiplication, that there will be duplication of effort and confusion? There may be, and we should think in terms of some strategy and co-ordinated structure for our initiatives, and those of other denominations. One such programme is called DAWN ('Discipling a Whole Nation'). More information about this will be found in Appendix A at the end of this book.

In chapter 13 George Lings explains that in 1985, there was one church plant per month. In 1990, there were 50% more: eighteen to twenty plants. Perhaps in 1991 there will be one per fortnight. I would like to think that before long, there will be one per week. With 43 dioceses, that would be not much more than one per diocese. Expressed as only one new church per 500 parishes, it hardly could be described as a 'baby boom'! My prayer is that *Planting New Churches* will assist, in some small way, this and greater goals.

PART ONE

Ecclesiology and Mission

CHAPTER ONE

Church Planting, Ecclesiology and Mission

George Carey, Archbishop of Canterbury

We were fortunate to be able to have the new Archbishop with us at this conference, within a month of his enthronement. We owe this to his having made it a priority, despite all the pressures of his other new commitments. Dr George Carey was with us for most of the morning and had made it a condition of coming that he gave the opening keynote address on this topic. Clearly this not only gave the most wonderful introduction to the day but is also the perfect foundation for this book. Here, the new denominational leader of our national church, on taking up his office, sets out his under-standing of the place and significance of church planting in the Church of England as he leads us in a decade of evangel-ism. He also pulls no punches in challenging both those committed to church planting and those within the structure; and he spells out issues and questions that we need to face together. Many of the other contributions included here, whether stories of plants or discussion of principles, illustrate both the potential and the challenges that our new Arch-bishop presented to us.

Dr Carey has given us this helpful blend of encouragement and challenge through much of the recent development of the church planting movement within the Church of England.

He attended two of our previous day conferences as Bishop of Bath and Wells, giving the main address in 1988, and chairing the event in 1989. He also contributed two different articles on the subject, one for thè Church of England News- paper *(20th October 1989) and one for the* Church Growth Digest *(Year 10, Issue 2, Winter 1988/89).*

Archbishop George was principal of Trinity College Bristol before becoming Bishop of Bath and Wells. Before that, among many other things, he was Vicar of St Nicholas church in the centre of Durham from 1975–1982. Whilst this was not an experience of church planting, under his leadership there the church turned right around and experienced rapid growth. It also developed a significant ministry into the City of Durham.

In his book The Church in the Market Place, *George Carey tells how he and his wife Eileen were able to prove what a strategic effect a dynamic church could have at the heart of urban life. This experience must play a part in his enthusiasm to see the multiplication of many more energetic, incarnational mission churches. To put it in his own words 'I am convinced that church planting is a mark of vigorous and outgoing Christianity and is a sign of hope for the future' (*CEN article, 20th October, 1989*); 'We must renew the church, moving out of our buildings into the community' (*Sunday Times, 13th January 1991*).*

What is church planting? The term seems to suggest a building; but that is not the case. In most cases, church planting is rather the planting of Christians in an area where the Christian presence is weak. In a previous paper I gave this definition:

> It is the transfer of part of a congregation in an area of need with the evangelistic expectation that new people will find faith and the renewal of their spiritual lives.

They could be planted in another church building, but

it is just as likely to be a secular building – a pub, a community centre and even a doctor's surgery or a home with a large lounge.

But why all the fuss about church planting? After all, there have been examples throughout Christian history. Ian Bunting was doing something like it in Durham in the seventies without causing any over-reaction. Many parishes have started congregations on new estates within their boundaries, meeting first in schools (one I heard of met in a garage!) before putting up a church building. By such means many daughter churches began, some of which are now parish churches. The congregation was created first, often a plant from the parish congregation itself. The bricks and mortar came later. I will return to this dynamic of church growth below.

One likely reason for the current interest is the conditions now prevailing, which make church planting a relevant and helpful model of discipling. First, the mood in the church suggests we are ready for new initiatives. The Lambeth Conference of 1988 must be seen as recording this new mood, as the bishops demanded a massive shift in mission orientation throughout the Communion. The resolutions did not ignore social concern or pastoral care but emphasised the priority of evangelism as underscoring other aspects of mission.

This Lambeth Conference was an expression of a remarkable ecumenical convergence of opinion, that the final decade of the second millennium should be a time of proclaiming faith in our risen Lord. To be sure, there are different agendas and different understandings at work. For some, it is plain, unadulterated preaching of the gospel which is required. For others it is celebration which will draw in new people by the sheer attractiveness of a faith expressed in worship and witness. For others still it means evangelising those who are already evangelised but do not look it. There is also the recovery of the lapsed – one of the targets of the Roman Catholic Decade of Evangelisation and perhaps the most difficult task of all.

Alongside this is the plain fact that the church on the corner with its traditional patterns of ecclesiastical life does not seem to pull in the customers. Whereas the church plants of the fifties on new estates were mirror images of the life of the nearby parish church, now the plants seem to allow a new freedom. That is part of their attractiveness, and it is not surprising when they run into conflict with the Church of England's structures.

The sweeping changes in society, resulting in different kinds of communities from the ones which shaped our towns and villages, mean that we are more mobile, more urban, more individualistic and more critical than previous generations. We are less likely to be influenced by what our parents and grandparents believed and thought. So religion is less likely to be a matter of culture, and more one of choice. Even so, the impact of peer group pressure is enormous in religion as in anything else. Young people especially like to think of themselves as non-conforming to earlier generations or what they think of as blinkered tradition; yet not conforming to the expectation of your peers is very testing indeed. That is why it is so difficult for many people to break into the Christian community from outside, for they are often moving from one sort of peer group to another. It is also the reason why many evangelicals who often talk about outreach actually spend most of their time with other evangelicals.

Despite all that, there is no evidence that modern people need God less; there is still wistfulness for a genuine spirituality. Many would agree with Sir Neville Mott who wrote recently:

I believe it is better and more interesting and fulfilling to build a personal faith in our historic, religious tradition than to throw it away and start again in the arid plains of atheism.[1]

So then, why church planting? Willy Sutton the American gangster, when asked why he robbed banks, replied: 'Because that is where the money is.' The church planter, likewise, could say: 'Because that is where people are; away from historical forms of Christianity, in their homes and clubs, and there we must go.'

The Theology of Church Planting

Our Anglican understanding of the church is rooted in episcopal leadership and parochial structure. This is not authoritarian oversight but leadership of God's mission to take the love of Christ into the world and to build up his church. Historically, episcopacy is arguably the most ancient of church orders. It is clearly evidenced in the foundation of our church. Gregory the Great sent Augustine to evangelise Britain and after planting the church Augustine returned to the continent to be consecrated Bishop of the English by St Virgilius. The parochial structure of our country followed soon after the foundation of the church. Theodore of Tarsus, an archbishop from Asia, must surely be one of the most remarkable archbishops of all time. It was he who structured the parish base of our church, rooting its missionary concern in pastoral care and regular worship. It was he who saw that by dividing the country up into districts or parishes, the form of the church could be given local expression. He thus gave utterance to an incarnational view of the church: that wherever a person might be in our land, there he or she can receive the benefits of the church and gain hope and challenge. There in the local, worshipping church, we can receive the grace of the sacraments; there in the preaching of the word, we can be built up in faith. There was far more to this, of course. The physical building was more, far more than a mere building: it stood as a visible sign of God's presence. As Michael Nazir-Ali writes:

> The parochial system has been instrumental in creating a meaningful Christian presence in an effective way and made the church approachable and familiar.[2]

But the question we face is whether this familiar presence is or can be made to be an effective tool of proclaiming faith in God in a modern world.

The deficiencies are all too obvious. What might have been possible for one clergyman and a congregation in maintaining an effective Christian presence in a small rural parish is hardly possible in an urban one of 10,000 souls – and there are many far larger units than that. The thin surpliced line of readers and clergy is stretched to breaking point in all our dioceses, deaneries and parishes.

Church planting therefore appears to offer attractive possibilities, because it is a way by which a more successful church with energetic lay people can help a neighbouring parish which has fallen on hard times. However, the planting of congregations in someone else's parish, deanery or even diocese prompts important theological questions, many of them raised sharply in David Pytches' and Brian Skinner's recent book *New Wineskins* (Eagle, 1991). What theological criteria should control our response?

Co-operation

First, I applaud the genuine motive in church planting, to be a tool at the service of the kingdom of God. Parish boundaries are not meant to be separate kingdoms, yet too often there can be an unhealthy competitiveness between parishes. A parish church which, for whatever reason, falls on hard times in its congregational life may find some of the vigorous Christians living within its boundaries worshipping at nearby lively churches. Our mobility has made us more eclectic and we can 'opt out' when the going gets tough. And there is an understandable attractiveness in belonging to a large and lively Christian community.

My hope, however, is that the dynamic of church planting might lead to great co-operation across parish boundaries, and that people might move back to worship in their immediate locality, not in ones and twos but as a body. Christian witness in a local community is not helped when our worshipping lives are conducted miles away from where we live.

There are a number of factors which stand in the way of this co-operation. One of them is the abuse of the parson's freehold. It does seem from one point of view an iniquitous misuse of privilege if the parson's freehold prevents outreach into the community. While the majority of our clergy are hard-working, conscientious men and women, there are sometimes people who have lost their way and who may resist the help of other Christian groups. That is one argument for the end of freehold, or at least some reform of it, because its very independency paralyses the mission of the church – freezing episcopal leadership and cutting off lay participation. In some situations, instead of episcopal leadership there is a despotic form of congregationalism. Such cases are few, but they do happen.

Nevertheless, as things stand at the moment it is wrong, legally and morally, if an Anglican church unilaterally decides to muscle in on another parish. While the motive may be honourable, the very act of setting up shop in another parish does nothing to build up a sense of cooperation. Rather the reverse: it may even weaken good work being done in the name of Christ and undermine the ministry of a fellow minister and congregation.

Identification

Second, the need to 'inculturate' the gospel must be borne in mind. The temptation is to assume that what God has blessed and is blessing in one place will be equally good next door. But it doesn't work out that way. At the human level, worship is a curious amalgam of personality, gifts, class structure, relationships and experience; to say nothing of the slow building of congregational life which may take generations. To believe that we can instantly create the same kind of experience which launched the church planting vision is a mistake. This needs to be heeded carefully because many involved in church planting have been heavily influenced by charismatic renewal, and there may be the innocent idea that all that is required is faithfulness to the vision and all will be well.

The biblical pattern of ministry is that of dying:

> Except a grain of wheat falls into the ground and dies, it abides alone, but if it dies it bears much fruit (John 12:24 NEB).

There is a cost involved in any real identification with the people we seek to minister to. The moment a congregation is planted in an area, there is commitment to that area; to its problems of lostness, to the soullessness of modern life, to the silent cries of the unemployed and the muted screams of the helpless. We dare not go with our own ideas of what they want. We must listen to what they are asking of us. If the church is to root itself in the real community then it must reflect that community, and this will not be easy.

In fact, church planting is ideally positioned to reflect that concern. Society appears to have turned its back on the sacralisation of life. In cathedrals where hundreds mill around, I have often wondered how many have any concept of sacred space; that in a place made valid by prayer they are standing on sacred ground. The glorious sounds of choir and organ may ring around them, but are perhaps remote and cerebral. By contrast, it is the home, the community centre, the place where the informal group can meet for coffee or for some singing from the music group, that can seem more immediate and accessible.

This is well understood, and is one of the reasons behind the growth of the house church movement. But it must not too quickly be assumed that sacralisation of space is dead and gone; nor that these two approaches are rivals and not allies. Do two million people visit Canterbury Cathedral every year just because it is an ancient building? I have personal evidence from my experience of Wells Cathedral, of people who in Karl Rahner's words were 'unmusical in religion' finding there and in them a refrain which has led them to the living God, through the tranquillity of a holy place. In a society when it is so easy for a person to feel overwhelmed by the pressure of life, the local church – open, attractive and accessible – still embodies Theodore's principle, the proclamation that 'We are here for you.'

Anglicanism

Third, what are the tangible symbols of Anglicanism in a church planting context? For example, how is an Anglican church plant distinguished from a nonconformist one? There is a worrying tendency to cut corners on Anglican ways of worship. The service may thus be free and easy, with little or no liturgy and few robes. But this obscures important marks of identification. In a highly mobile society, the people who come to faith in one place, and then move away, should be grafted into church life elsewhere, and must be helped to belong to a wider group than one intimate and local circle. They must feel part of a national church and a worldwide Anglican family.

There is an attractive immediacy about simple, unaffected worship; but when people meet God they enter upon a journey which takes them more and more into his mystery. Worship erupts and results from encounter. The emerging love relationship can, and often does, lead to a dissatisfaction with 'wordy', kerygmatic Christianity. History demonstrates how many evangelicals have moved 'up the candle' to embrace a wider catholicism. So, what place has the numinous – quietness, beauty, waiting – in a church plant? The anxiety not to be fettered by tradition is understood, but history demonstrates that any group quickly creates traditions of its own. No-one is free from tradition, and if there is (as all church planting literature suggests) a desire to be biblical, then precedence, history and Anglican practice must be taken seriously.

The Way Forward

1. Strategy
The time will shortly come when bishops will have to develop a strategy for church planting. Initiatives which advance beyond parish boundaries should not be left for DIY enthusiasts. Such a strategy will start from a partnership between the local church and the wider church represented by the bishop. On the one

hand, a large church might wish to say to its bishop: 'We are here to be a resource: how can we be used by the wider church?' The response must of necessity be limited by geography, but the willingness to be used would be welcomed. On the other hand, there is the bishop's vision for his diocese. Where are the areas in which the church is weak or under-represented? What churches might be able to contribute to the life of those places? There are now positive examples available of just such a spirit of co-operation between an active local church and the wider fellowship.

2. Authority
The authority of a bishop is there not to quench the Spirit but to recognise what God is doing and to allow for the exercise of ministry in the wider church. The bishop has to ensure that the ministry leadership of the local church is properly trained and thoroughly Anglican in its approach. This is not to argue for a rigid conformity; variety of traditions has always been a mark of Anglican comprehensiveness. But the question of where authority is located is important, especially if in reality it resides not with the bishop but with the parent church.

3. Church Planting as Extension
Church planting is a tool of mission, not the final purpose of mission. It is not a replacement for the parish church, but an extension of its life. That is why I strongly encourage all parishes of moderate size to consider church planting in their own area. It must be done carefully and prayerfully. But it can be done by a committed group of people who believe they have something to share in an area of the parish. For example, fewer and fewer churches have evening services, and the drift of people becoming 'oncers' is to be regretted. But if there is no great enthusiasm for evensong,

there is scope for growing Sunday evening congregations, with Agape meals, house churches on housing estates, and so forth.

4. Every Member Ministry
One of the strengths of church planting is that it takes seriously evangelism by the whole church working together, and particularly by lay people. An enormous amount of commitment is required by any group which covenants to leave the security of a larger fellowship for a ministry which for months and years may not be particularly fruitful. But the rewards can also be very great.

5. Ecumenical Consultation
No attempt should be made at church planting without considering the ecumenical implications. Anglicans cannot afford the luxury of thinking that what is done in their patch is their own affair. Any new venture will affect other Christians: Baptists, Methodists, or whoever is working in the area. Others must be consulted and drawn into the planning, so that even where they may not agree with the vision, they may understand why it is being carried forward.

Conclusion

The Church of England must grow stronger. As a church inextricably linked with the constitution of our land it is in an unrivalled position of trust and influence. There is a new confidence abroad; the sap is rising, and new life is flowing. Church planting, along with other initiatives, has great potential as an exciting and positive resource for the church, and the fulfilling of that potential is my hope and my prayer.

PART TWO

Church Planting in Practice

In the second section we will look at a whole range of different case histories of recent Anglican church plants in England. These studies illustrate the wide variety and creativity which is developing in response to the many very different church situations on the one hand and the diverse community and cultural contexts on the other.

On page 15 of the Introduction, I described seven broad categories of church planting. These stories provide examples of most of these broad types of initiative. On the previous page of the Introduction I also proposed three identifying characteristics of the essence of a church plant: *mission multiplication*, and *incarnation*. In introducing the first few stories I will highlight these aspects of each planting project, but from then on I will leave it to the reader to look for these key qualities in the narrative told by each church planter.

I believe that each study is an authentic case of church planting evangelisation and that we can learn much from the ways that each went about their mission challenge. The qualities of sacrifice and commitment are also often not far from the surface.

CHAPTER TWO

Pioneering on a Council Estate

Ann Wooderson

Perhaps one of the most striking areas of unreached, un-churched communities in our country are the many council estates. These are all the more easily overlooked when they are set in parishes with plenty of owner-occupied housing. Many a vicar has a sense of failure due to the low or insignificant representation in his congregation from the public housing sector. This may still be true after many efforts to evangelise the residents of such estates. Of course it is a different matter if the parish is almost exclusively public/corporation housing — then the mission task is clear and unavoidable, although often still very difficult. However, many thriving parish churches seem to be almost completely unaware that they are totally failing to reach those on the council estate. Their very success in other neighbourhoods can blind them to this mission challenge.

*There are now many encouraging examples of Anglican church plants which have responded to this opportunity. Our first case study is of such a plant on a council estate in the Midlands. As we look for the three identifying characteristics of church plants, we have already established how this venture has an immediately apparent **mission** motivation. Since the project led to a new community of faith with a Sunday* *worship service on the estate it is also clearly producing* **multiplication** *of church life.*

This case study is described by the church planter involved, Ann Wooderson. For many years she had partnered her husband Michael in his ministry in Morden, then in Aldridge and latterly in Chasetown parish in Staffordshire. It was in Aldridge in 1974 that they pioneered the new approach to evangelism called 'Good News Down Your Street'. This has now been successfully applied in many different churches. Ann explains how it has been a key evangelistic strategy in her church plant. It was in 1985 that friends convinced Ann that she should leave her nursing job and train for the ministry in her own right. She was ordained deacon in 1989 and her first assignment was to be licensed for 2 years to work in the council estate at Glascote Heath near Tamworth – some 15 miles from her husband's parish. This somewhat forgotten area was the nearest opportunity that the diocese could find for Ann. Obviously she could not move to live on the estate, so the **incarnation** *quality of the plant was first evident in the depth of her work 'on the ground'. She undertook foot-slogging round the doors to meet people and build relationships. This continued for a year before any worship service was held and in this respect it was a more incarnational approach than those cases where the first step is to start Sunday worship for people on an estate. Furthermore, this story shows how the whole thrust of Ann's mission was to express the life of the emerging church into every aspect of the life of the council estate.*

It is appropriate that the illustration in this first case study deals with another common historic Anglican blind spot – since the leader was a woman. Ann Wooderson was a team of one, pioneering on her own, when she led this plant out onto a very tough estate. The UK church even at its strongest is weak at reaching unchurched men – but there was a row of burly miners and working men (one with a large earring in the shape of a cross) among the 22 lined up for the bishop to confirm just after Ann wrote this story. For church plants that stagnate or never seem to grow, there are lessons here about the priority of evangelism and an evangelistic approach that works. Of course Ann is not unique – other women have led church plants onto council estates. Several are Church Army sisters and at least one other I know is a clergy wife like Ann. Other stories are also told in this book by women involved in leading different sorts of planting. The leadership and ministry gifts of both women and the laity are finding many new means of expression in Anglican church planting in every sort of situation.

The Background

In the late sixties or early seventies, Glascote Heath was targeted for the building of a new estate to accommodate large numbers of displaced families from Birmingham, along with some local families. About 1,200 residences were built, to accommodate around 5,000 people. A centre contained several shops, a health centre, library, community centre, two primary schools and one high school. To the east of the estate, a number of owner-occupied properties were built, for a further 2,000 people. These 7,000 people became an extension to the parish of Glascote, and the responsibility of the parish of St George's. The new estate became of prime concern to the church, yet no lasting inroads were made.

The families originally sent to the Heath were young marrieds with children. In time, these people became grandparents, many still living together with their children and sometimes their children's children. There is a high incidence of single parenting among the young teenagers: often, a daughter will conceive out of wedlock to provide her mother, in raising the child for her, with a *raison d'être*. The children's fathers are conspicuous by their absence. Unemployment is high, and all the consequent social problems are present. Nevertheless, there is a sense of community, and there are many large and happy families.

There is a large, new, multi-purpose Roman Catholic church on the perimeter of the estate, although the priest is not resident. At the time of my arrival, in July 1989, a number of faithful people from St George's were holding a monthly family service, mainly for the uniformed organisations, in the community centre. But however bright and entertaining the services were, those organising them were still seen as visitors to the area. The organisational burden was heavy; and when a new incumbent arrived at St George's in 1990, the services ceased in the interests of making progress at St George's itself. After St George's pulled out, I maintained a low-key monthly family service, simply to avoid giving the impression that the church had lost interest.

On the next large estate, two miles away, a brand new church and multi-purpose community centre had been built: St Martin's Stoneydelph. In July 1989 I was appointed assistant curate at St Martin's, with the intention of working primarily on Glascote Heath. In November 1990 the Heath officially became part of a team ministry with St George's and St Martin's.

Beginnings

I began with no strategy. I had an overwhelming sense of isolation and bewilderment, which was in fact vital in equipping me for the task as I learnt to depend on God. All the uniformed organisations were disbanded because of a lack of local leadership; all that was left was one small group meeting to pray for the Heath. Two of them actually lived there, and hope began to be rekindled.

There was a lot of pressure for me, as a clergy person, to commence weekly services. I held out against this, both from lack of energy and from lack of actual believers, and looking back I see this was a major part of God's strategy.

Over the first months I followed up every contact, doing everything personally and very little by telephone. It seemed of vital importance that the parish should realise that it did indeed have its own minister. Most of the work seemed fruitless and very time-consuming. Often there were social problems needing time and practical help. If there had been a church service at that stage, the temptation to invite them to attend would have been enormous, and the help people received would have had church attendance as a perceived price tag.

There was much discouragement. One morning after two more particularly awful visits I felt ready to give up. God might well love the Heath; but the Heath certainly did not love him. It seems that at our weakest places God is able to show us his purposes most clearly. As I prayed, I saw a huge wall on all sides of me with no top or bottom. I saw my own hands scrabbling frantically at this wall, attempting to remove some of the bricks, but all that happened was that my hands became torn and bleeding. Then I saw God's hand gently remove six bricks, and then one by one bunches of brightly coloured lilies grew out from the gaps. When all six of the spaces were filled with flowers, he gathered them together and placed them into a gold vase under a church archway. I came to understand that the work of removing the bricks was God's work, not mine, and that when there were six whole households of believers, it would be the time to gather together in one place to worship as a church on the Heath.

In due course I had a number of people who wanted to think through some aspects of faith. I was ill-equipped to instruct them all personally, so I imported six people to lead and resource six *Good News*[1] teams. Enormous negotiation was required to establish them; but in October 1989 the first six homes received teams. Eight people came to faith and joined the life of our fellowship as a result.

I gathered these people together to lead them on, through a Nurture Group. The aim of this group was to link people together as new Christians; to help them adjust to group work; to move them on in their faith; and to discover their gifts and abilities. These new Christians then went out to other homes wishing to receive a team. This has been our most significant means of promoting growth, and in eighteen months 41 people came to faith as a result.

Not having a weekly Sunday service, the developing fellowship became hungry for worship, and we began meeting together. We shared Agape meals, as very few were confirmed, and used some of the lovely services from the fellowship at Iona. We worked through a course on Christian love, and then moved on to do the *Saints Alive* course. Praying together is a large hurdle for new Christians, so we formed prayer triplets as well as praying as a group.

Towards the end of the summer term, the group began to feel a need to reach out to some of the 3,000 young people in the area. We launched a summer holiday club called 'The Lion, the Witch and the Wardrobe'. This was run primarily by the new Christians. Two of the young mothers started their faith journey through the work, along with a number of children. Over 60 children attended, and some 35 now attend a weekly Friday evening event called 'Aslan's Gang'.

The Church Begins

In response to God's vision given many months previously, when six entire households were in the fellowship we began weekly worship as a church, using the community centre. We hung our banners over the graffiti, and adjusted quickly to the smell of the toilets! Numbers were very sparse initially, and even those who had come to faith found it difficult to associate with 'church'. It had never been a part of their culture. Many have bridged the gap, but it is necessary in this work to realise how enormous is the cultural gap for the unchurched.

We needed a name, and after much prayer 'St Peter's on the Heath' seemed the most appropriate. Under the Heath was the rocky coal face; and St Peter the Rock seemed most appropriate. After the church was named it took on a new identity, and a new sense of worth and purpose.

There were various difficulties in creating a community of believers. The first was cultural. These people are committed to their family, not to their neighbour. Often, there are long-term feuds to overcome that have ruled their lives for years. 'Loving your neighbour' is a new and unwelcome concept. The only group they have related to is the family group.

A relatively small number of households are a 'normal' family unit. In that sense, immorality is the norm. Consequently for most an awareness of sin and repentance comes after the encounter with the love of God, not before. It is useless and sometimes destructive to present them first with the Ten Commandments, although some would want to do so.

Having no format to follow, our worship pattern has had to evolve. A family service is essential, but there is a need to have some quieter worship as well, and the Eucharist (even to an unconfirmed gathering) is surprisingly important and central. Sometimes a guest priest celebrates; but the more usual pattern is for me to lead the whole service omitting the Eucharistic Prayer. A friend brings the consecrated bread and wine from the simultaneous service at St George's, which we then share.

Fourteen were confirmed in 1990; and a further 22 were confirmed in May 1991. Naturally, adult baptism has become part of the life of St Peter's, although it is not always easy to perform. An evening service was never considered, as few people would venture out after dark. Our times of worship are good, involving all ages.

Resources

Initially, any outlay came from a fund of around £200, which had been collected over the years specifically for the Heath. St Martin's gave me a £30 allowance for petrol each month; otherwise the work had to be self-sufficient (if there is such a thing for Christians). Family Service collections were a very meagre £10-£12, which at least covered the cost of hiring the community centre. The school would have been better for worship, but proved too costly to hire on a regular basis.

During the first year, we managed to maintain the practical financial requirements and meet some of the social needs in the community. This depended on the generosity of those who had anything to give, and some very helpful gifts from other congregations. We gave out hampers at Christmas and arranged a day out in the Spring for some of the single parent mothers and children.

After the advent of our weekly worship, some people

have begun to tithe. The giving is very healthy considering the poverty of some of the congregation, averaging around £250 per month.

Resources of people as well as finance are vital. Many busy men and women gave both time and abilities. Some came to speak at the Family Service; others provided leaders for our Good News teams; and one trained lay reader felt a call to channel his efforts and gifts into the Heath. We learned a great deal about sharing and pooling the resources available.

Problems Encountered

1. Evil
The Heath is a place alive with all kinds of evil, both practised and inherited. One family approached me because they and their five children had all seen, at different times, the manifestation of a dead miner, who was killed in the shaft below the house. There were dramatic ways by which this could have been dealt with, but too much drama was already accredited to the evil one. As the family one by one gave their lives to the Lord, all manifestations ceased, the husband found work after nine years of unemployment, and all five children were baptised. God received much praise, and the enemy very little attention.

2. Poverty
The poor, hungry, oppressed and damaged persons were ever a priority with Jesus. He was as much involved with people's social and physical problems as with their spiritual needs. So we too must work among people, meeting them where their needs are and loving them into the kingdom.

One of the things I learned early on was that it is not acceptable to give 'charity' to people's needs. Their dignity is important. For example, when a church nearby gave us a van-load of good clothing for the Heath, we devised a way of selling them for a nominal cost. The whole project was a huge success, and I am constantly being asked: 'When are we having another *New for You*?'

3. Loneliness

There were a number of single parents, lonely, some on the breadline, attempting to fill long days with purpose. One of the young women, herself the mother of three, formed a group to work through our *Good News* course and then used the group as a base for working with mothers and toddlers.

The Future

Once or twice the congregation has been too large for the hall. We have squeezed almost 100 people in, but it can comfortably hold around 80. Something must be done to enable future growth as we continue to reach out into the community.

One suggestion is that we take over the management of the community centre, with the hope that we could extend it. However, the local council is not enthusiastic, and the property has little potential. Another possible solution is to use an area above the main worship area in the local Roman Catholic church. This would meet the needs of St Peter's, and also lend some integrity to the unity of the church working at Glascote Heath. However, for the time being our average weekly attendance of around 50 adults and children fits comfortably where we are.

The work through Aslan's Gang looks after children up to the age of twelve to thirteen years, but not beyond. What we have done at present is to encourage the teenagers who come our way to become helpers in the children's work, as well as befriending them. More is needed, and two of the new Christians (although parents themselves) are both just 21, and want to help and lead some youth work. Despite the energy required, we will need to press on with something for the 3,000 young people in the area.

Leadership training will be important. Discovering gifts and abilities releases people in a constructive and purposeful way, to be themselves for the good of the body and the family to which they belong. Some obvious leadership gifts are emerging, although there needs to be an awareness of balance, so as not to push people too quickly into too much responsibility. A recent holiday at Spring Harvest was a real time of growth. In the light of the temporariness of my appointment, it is vital to encourage and train leadership.

Two areas of concern have become clear to me. First, the lack of people prepared to work out their ministries in the difficult and less pleasant areas. Before coming to Glascote Heath, I would have included myself in that category. Second, the lack of expectancy in the Church of England that much would happen as a result of this church plant, and the little planning given to the long-term care and welfare of such a congregation.

Conclusions

Real Christianity is contagious, a living thing spread from person to person through the Holy Spirit. When the church is functioning as Christ would wish, the Holy Spirit works not only in the growth of each member of the body, but also in prompting those around who witness to the aliveness of the life in

Christ. Worship is central, and it is in such times that we find the resources to face the world.

I am left with many questions. The context into which we seek to share the good news of Jesus is sometimes one of hopelessness, poverty and purposelessness. Government policy on various issues, instead of building and encouraging, is too often the weapon by which people are rendered powerless. Families are undermined, and because of poverty and materialism, money becomes a twentieth-century god. Stealing is a way of life (the vicarage has been burgled twice).

Yet in the midst of all these problems, Jesus continues to change people and bring them a divine perspective on their lives. The circumstances are not always changed, but the Holy Spirit within changes attitudes and brings hope and joy. Out of a personal commitment to God comes a vision of commitment to community and others, which ultimately must make a difference.

CHAPTER THREE

Multiple Congregations at St Thomas, Crookes

Derek Frank

In my Introduction I explained that many instances of developing multiple parallel congregations share the essence of church planting. St Thomas, Crookes is a church which has pursued this pattern very creatively over the past five years. In this relatively short period it has developed four congregations. Derek Frank explains how Robert Warren conceived and implemented this vision. Derek is one of the four congregational leaders; he joined the staff team at St Thomas in 1987 when he and his wife Francoise moved from a curacy at Clay Cross in Derbyshire.

*Let us see how the development of these four congregations relates to my analysis of the essence of church planting. Firstly, St Thomas is obviously **multiplying** church life based on different congregational leaders, leadership teams, ministeries and home group structures. In this they may have gone further than some satellite congregational plants which, although meeting on Sunday in different buildings, still maintain a single structure of home groups with mixed members from different congregations, and have less differentiated leadership and ministry patterns. The real multiplying essence of St Thomas, Crookes is shown by the fact that a fifth congregation is now emerging. A momentum seems to* *have been generated by this intentional pattern of natural reproduction.*

*Secondly, they have developed an increasingly clear **mission** emphasis. The original motivation for multiplying congregations back in 1985 may have come principally from a desire to continue the growth in numbers at St Thomas. However, as plans evolved, this mission to reach more individuals progressed to a strategy of using each service to reach different groups of people. In the two morning service congregations the differences may be quite subtle – with the 9.15 am service having more of an emphasis on young families and small children and the 11.15 am service being more geared to adults and older folk. However, the differentiation becomes more marked in the two evening services, with students and 20's at 6.30 pm with the 9.00 pm service aimed at a quite different group that the church has failed to reach at all in the UK. Derek Frank describes this congregation as a mission to 'urban culture'. This has included a focus on the night club community in Sheffield and people who might be described as 'punk' or of alternative lifestyle.*

*The **incarnational** character of these multiplying congregations may be less immediately evident when their Sunday worship is expressed in the same building. However, we have already noted that church planting takes the emphasis off a building-centred and Sunday-service-centred church.*

The Nine O'Clock service may most easily demonstrate the incarnational aspects of these plants through their 'whole of the week' church life and ministry. Incarnation is occurring through the initial contact-making and relationship-building in the places where those in this 'urban culture' group live, work and socialise. It is then taken further by the committed discipling in small groups. These are now helping hundreds who were previously right outside the sphere of traditional church life. The groups aim to help them work out how their new-found Christian faith can be applied to their own context. This illustrates that incarnation is not just about geography and location, but is also about reaching different cultures and communities.

This chapter also tells how the Nine O'Clock service congregation may relocate to a different building to make way

*for the most recently arrived – the Sunday Night Live –
congregation. I believe that this makes evident that these St
Thomas congregations are in every sense church plants – the
location being purely a matter of practical consideration.*

The planting of multiple congregations within the
same building, such as at St Thomas, Crookes in Sheffield, may seem to be a rather specialised aspect of
church planting that only relates to larger churches.
However, the insights discovered do in fact have a
broader relevance to any expanding church.

The Setting

St Thomas presently has between 1,000 and 1,500
people attending each Sunday. The church is in a
suburb of Sheffield in South Yorkshire – which,
according to the recent MARC Europe church census,
has the lowest percentage of adults attending church
in the country. A recent survey of the diocese of Sheffield showed that average church congregations have
fewer than 100 attending, with one in three churches
drawing fewer than 50, and only six churches drawing
more than 200.

By those standards, St Thomas stands out favour-
ably. However, some research carried out by the
Bishop of Sheffield has shown that 100 years ago,
within the city of Sheffield alone, there were 25
churches with an attendance of over 500, of which nine
were over 1,000 and two were over 2,500. So by those
standards, St Thomas is rather less successful than
present-day statistics would suggest. The only real
claim St Thomas may dare to make is that it is one of
the few churches in Sheffield that is larger today than
it was 100 years ago. Then, as one of the middle-sized

churches in Sheffield, attendance was around the 600 mark; but as in so many other churches it subsequently fell to well under 100.

The story of the recovery of St Thomas back up to 600 by the early eighties, and then a further increase to 1,200 since, has been told in Robert Warren's book *In the Crucible* (1989). This tells how growth began under the leadership of Michael Cole from 1964–1971, when numbers rose to about 250, and then under Robert's leadership, reaching 600 by the early eighties. During this time there had been a major renovation of the church building costing over £600,000, a move into charismatic renewal, and the launch of a Local Ecumenical Project with the Baptists. There were some internal difficulties, but much development had taken place and the momentum of growth was maintained.

However, as the 600 level was reached, the organisation of the church started becoming cumbersome and impersonal as the original systems were outgrown. If, for example, some children's work leaders need recruiting, the size of the church made it impossible to know who the likely people might be (or for that matter, who should be avoided). Letters would be sent to fellowship group leaders asking them to suggest names. Things felt increasingly bureaucratic, and the sense of being a church family was fading. Although growth hadn't completely stopped, it was clear that unless a way through was found, a plateau not far beyond 600 would be reached as the mood of the church became: 'Help, stop, we're too big already!'

Even so, being a larger church offered benefits which were still worth pursuing. Resources had become available to make it possible to undertake ventures that a smaller church would find hard to contemplate. Economies of scale were emerging through the centralised management of the church. The size of the church was an encouragement to those inside as well as those outside. Yet the sense of personal relationship – of knowing and being known – which the smaller church can offer more effectively, was being missed. A means of keeping and indeed recovering the advantages of the smaller church was needed.

Celebration or Congregation?

During this time, Robert visited John Wimber's Anaheim Vineyard. While worshipping there amongst several thousand others, he was struck by the enjoyment of celebration that seems to be instinctive to Americans. The fact that few people knew the person sitting next to them did not seem to matter: given the American personality, they would by the end of the service. This was in contrast to the English preference for congregation rather than celebration, through which the sense of longer-term relationship can more easily be expressed. Robert considered the possibility of hiring a bigger auditorium in order to use larger-scale celebration to sustain growth; but God's leading to rebuild St Thomas at such cost made this seem inappropriate. Instead, structures needed to be built around the people. This meant separate congregations, each with their own relational identities and growth potential, yet with a common sense of identity that from time to time could be expressed in whole-church celebration.

There were reasons for those congregations being in the same building. The geographical size of the parish of Crookes is small: all points are within ten minutes' walk from the church. Daughter churches were ruled out by this compactness of the parish. Further, neither the leadership nor the vast majority of the church had any desire or sense of call from God to divide. The

Baptists had already demolished their building following the launch of the LEP: it made little sense now to plant further small churches in the area.

The experience of the LEP gave final shape to the model of separate congregations, each with their own leadership teams yet meeting in the same building. The episcopal one-man style of the Anglicans, and the congregational style of the Baptists, had been found to be mutually enriching. Even before the LEP, St Thomas had moved towards a more congregational kind of leadership through consultation during the building project. What now occurred to Robert was the possibility of going a stage further, and using the one form of church leadership St Thomas did not already have: presbyterian leadership through a team.

Developing Leadership through Teams

From these beginnings came the vision for congregations in St Thomas. Each was to have its own congregational leader, working with a leadership team that would share responsibility for the congregation. The life of each would aim to reflect its particular membership. As the congregation was to be self-contained, the leadership team was as follows:

1. A *congregational pastor*, responsible for the counselling and healing ministry within the congregation. Through a team of pastoral leaders, responsibility for the welcome of new members and the oversight of the congregation's fellowship groups.

2. An *organiser*, responsible for all the administrative aspects of services and social events.

3. A *ministry leader*, responsible for moving people in and out of the various ministries of the congregation.

4. A *worship team leader*, responsible for leading the worship team and developing worship.

While the leadership teams would need a degree of autonomy to develop the potential of their congregation, it was also important that the congregations be held together to avoid the church fragmenting. The picture of how to achieve this, which the Lord gave to Robert, was that of a piece of weaving with the warp and weft running in opposite directions. In effect, it was a picture of a leadership matrix, to maintain coordination across the congregations (see figure below).

Out of this emerged not only a leadership team for each congregation, but also a whole-church leadership team for each major area of the life of the church. For example, the team of congregational pastors could coordinate policy in the healing ministry. Consistency of worship could be maintained across the congregations through the worship team leaders meeting together, so that a regular worshipper in one congregation could attend another and still feel at home. Standard prac-

THE LEADERSHIP MATRIX

CONGREGATIONAL LEADERSHIP TEAMS	1	2	3	4	WHOLE CHURCH TEAMS
TEAM LEADER	X	X	X	X	STAFF TEAM
PASTORAL LEADER	X	X	X	X	PASTORAL TEAM
ORGANISER	X	X	X	X	ORGANISERS TEAM
MINISTRY LEADER	X	X	X	X	MINISTRY TEAM
WORSHIP LEADER	X	X	X	X	WORSHIP TEAM

tice regarding organisational matters could be maintained, and in the areas of ministry which needed to be handled on a whole-church basis (such as children's and youth work), a common approach could be exercised. Furthermore, a staff leadership team emerged comprising the congregational leaders.

With the way ahead clear, Robert took to the church council in January 1985 the idea of splitting the morning service into two in order to begin the journey into congregations. The idea was resisted, on the basis that there was already enough difficulty in organising one morning service, let alone two. Although Robert disagreed, it evidently was not the right time to press ahead. It was not until September 1987 that the move into congregations was made. By this time two important events had occurred: the Sheffield Wimber conference which had breathed new life into the church, and the start of the Nine O'Clock service. The result was a heart for change, and the basis for the launch of four congregations.

It is said that many over-estimate what can be done in one year, and under-estimate what can be done in five. This has been true in the subsequent experience of congregations. Although involving much more work to develop than first anticipated, their potential appears much greater than originally envisaged.

Team Ministry

The constitution of the staff team is vital. At the *Leading Larger Churches* conference in May 1989, a conversation with Eddie Gibbs (Professor of Church Growth at Fuller Seminary in Pasadena) proved crucial. He remarked that the Anglican system of using curates to bolster staff teams imposed an upper limit on church growth. Curates, however competent, are passing

through, and on their way want training for their
future role as generalists. Eddie Gibbs had noted a
common factor from worldwide observation of
churches which had sustained long-term growth: the
existence of a staff team willing as individuals to
specialise and to make a long-term commitment to the
church.

For St Thomas, this led to the idea of becoming
a legally constituted team ministry, in which each
congregation's leader would be a person of incumbent
status on a seven-year contract. In summer 1990, the
team ministry was officially instituted, providing for
team vicars at the two morning congregations, and
the Baptist minister at the 6.30 p.m. congregation.
The lay leader of the Nine O'Clock service is now in
training as an NSM, and Robert has become the rector
overseeing the church as a whole. In practice, this
means that whereas before people previously looked
to Robert as their vicar, they now look to their congregational leader as vicar. It's taken time to purge out
of the system the standard answer to any question
that posed difficulty, which was to 'ask Robert!' This
has been achieved by the Baptist minister looking
after the day-to-day running of the church, and each
staff member taking on specific whole-church responsibilities such as children's work, youth work and pastoral work. The occasional offices – not as infrequent
as their name suggests – are shared out. This releases
Robert into a more strategic role, including the oversight of each congregational leader. With a full-time
administrator, together with office staff and caretakers, St Thomas now has a structure capable of
handling further growth and development.

Impact to Date: Quantity

Some benefits of the congregational model are already well proven. Numerical growth has followed, by breaking the tendency to stagnate as services reach the 'church-full' level, normally reckoned to be around 85% of seating capacity. This is demonstrated in several ways:

1. Most dramatic has been the provision of a frame of reference for the Nine O'Clock service. In five years this has grown from an initial group of 50 up to as many as 500 on occasions.

2. The morning service, which was split to form the 9.15 a.m. and 11.15 a.m. congregations, has grown significantly. With a seating capacity of about 400, the morning service with children had for some years plateaued at the 'church-full' barrier. The split has resulted in a jump from an average of 320 children and adults in 1987, to a combined total now for the two morning congregations of 520.

3. By contrast, the 6.30 p.m. congregation had plateaued at the 'church-full' level of around 350 for the last five years. The loss of the forty who left to join the Nine O'Clock service is scarcely discernible in the statistics. The challenge is therefore to keep finding ways of releasing new congregations; and currently on a Sunday evening when the Nine O'Clock service is not using the church building, a new late-evening service known as 'Sunday Night Live' is being developed. This demonstrates the potential, under the umbrella of the congregational model, for multiplying further congregations, although the feeling is that one every four or five years is probably sufficient to cope with!

Impact to Date: Quality

Beyond the numerical growth, there is a growth in quality. Congregations are able to provide a greater sense of sharing life together, and services can be given a style which ministers to the particular needs of their members. For example, at the 9.15 a.m. congregation, where there are a large number of small children, everything from services to social events can be tailored accordingly. Older people are still very welcome, but there is freedom to focus on young families, knowing that the 11.15 a.m. service provides a style more appropriate to adults. 6.30 p.m. focuses on students and people in their twenties, and the Nine O'Clock service on urban culture. Relationships are thus more within natural social groupings, which enables a wide range of people to feel a close identification with the church.

Although the organisational structure is now bigger, the sense of bureaucracy has not increased in proportion. The hazard of the daughter church approach – requiring four sets of accounts, four Daughter Church Councils, and so on – are avoided, but the benefits of increased size are available. For example, each congregation has access to relatively sophisticated accounting and information systems, which would simply not be viable were the organisation not centralised.

There has been multiplication of leadership. One of the original concerns was whether there would be sufficient people capable of filling the new leadership roles. But a missionary visiting recently, who had belonged to the church when congregations were first proposed, remarked that he now knew hardly any of the people in congregational leadership. This suggests that there were more capable people in the church than the non-congregational structure had allowed to come forward.

For staff team members, there can be increased quality of ministry. The question might be asked: Does the warp and weft of the matrix leadership have double the strength, or twice the hassle? The answer to both is: Yes. For example, there is less freedom for congregational leaders than there would be for independent vicars, and there has to be a constant willingness to give ground in order to keep the church together. But being a staff team in one building has many benefits. Concerns about such matters as the church roof, the parish magazine and the occasional offices are greatly reduced. Energy and resources are released for what is the primary aim: the penetration of the kingdom of God.

The Future

There is considerable further potential to develop the multiple congregation model. What an 'expanded team-ministry' might mean is currently being explored, recognising that this could involve new congregations, on or off-site. The next stage of the journey will probably be for the Nine O'Clock service to move out, perhaps to a redundant church which need not be near St Thomas. The underlying principle is that the gospel cannot be preached effectively if the structures do not provide adequate room for those who come to faith. The aim is therefore not only to accommodate what is already happening, but also to provide for what could potentially happen.

Conclusion

Having been so positive about the benefits of developing multiple congregations, it must be noted that almost the first action Robert took 20 years ago was to merge the two morning services that then existed! Splitting congregations is not the panacea for every church growth problem: sometimes just the opposite is needed. But it is one demonstration of how constraints to growth can be removed, and as part of the overall mosaic of church growth, gives encouragement to believe that we could in our time see widespread numbers in church even in excess of those a hundred years ago.

CHAPTER FOUR

Reaching the Asian Community

Everyone recognises that the arrival and then the establishment of ethnic minority communities is a significant dimension of English urban life. Many Afro-Caribbean groups are Christian by background and have continued their own patterns of church life in England with their own traditional denominational streams. As Anglicans, our task in such cases is not so much church planting, but more to build bridges of fellowship and unity. We need to respect their church traditions, indigenous leadership and different expressions of worship and witness – while also seeking opportunities for appropriate partnership and interchange. These should both enrich each of the Christian churches but also effectively speak to the community around of the reconciling work of Jesus. In some circumstances the laying of these foundations of unity and sharing may bring to light opportunities to co-operate together in a church planting venture to reach the unchurched of either ethnic background.

In some of the Asian communities there are also those who are already Christian with their own church structures and some are pioneering excellent church planting initiatives among their nominal Christian and non-Christian neighbours. However, this is less common and there is more scope for Anglicans to consider whether God is calling them to the mission task of cross-cultural church planting. The next two stories are encouraging, if unspectacular examples of such endeavours. They illustrate well how church planting is almost the only viable evangelistic strategy in such cases. Experience has shown that crusades and evangelistic missions on their own bear little fruit in sharing Jesus with those of other faiths. Such enterprises must be part of an integrated plan to establish appropriate communities of faith, where multiplication is matched by incarnation. Our two examples are set in the very different areas of London suburbs and urban industrial Bolton. The Hounslow story is told by the vicar John Barter who conceived the vision and led the plan. On the other hand St Luke's Bolton were fortunate in having a lay couple linked to Interserve with experience of working with Asians. So Robin and Ros Holley were the obvious ones to lead and train the Bolton team.

I: The Experience of St Paul's Church, Hounslow

John Barter, Holy Trinity with St Paul's, Hounslow

The Background

Our parish is four miles east of Heathrow Airport, which dominates our life both from the point of view of noise and employment. We have a rapidly changing population. The elderly are moving away for peace and quiet, the materially successful are moving to more salubrious areas, and the young are moving away in search of cheaper housing. Their places are being filled with families of Asian background, coming South from Southall. Within the parish we have 5,000 children whose first language is Urdu or Punjabi, and many who would claim English as their first language but who are at home speaking Hindi, or a local Indian language. We now have, perhaps, 70% of our adult population and a much higher percentage of children originating from the Indian sub-continent. Naturally, Islam, Hinduism and Sikhism are the most common religions within our parish.

This rapidly changing population had a devastating effect on the parish of St Paul's, Hounslow. Its membership simply moved away, leaving a small and ageing congregation, unable to mount the kind of mission necessary. When the vicar of St Paul's retired, the parish was amalgamated with ours at Holy Trinity under a Pastoral Scheme, finalised in summer 1988. We now have one parish with two parish churches a mile apart: Holy Trinity, set in the town centre, and St Paul's, set in the residential area.

For a number of years, Holy Trinity has been concentrating its mission and ministry to the thousands of people who work and shop in the centre of our town. The result has been that our congregation, suffering like St Paul's from the exodus of its residents, has found that growth has come from an ever-wider area. It is a strong but eclectic congregation. This makes it difficult to be effective in the local community.

The Benefits of Having Two Churches

We are blessed with a church building which has been extensively re-ordered and refurbished for its mission to the town. Shortly, St Paul's will also have been rebuilt for its specific missionary task. There is an enormous advantage in having two churches: complementary patterns of worship can take place in each, without duplication. Soon after becoming responsible for St Paul's, we closed its main morning service and encouraged the residue of its congregation to join with us at Holy Trinity. This gave us a greater sense of unity within the parish, and also opened up the opportunity of starting something entirely different at St Paul's.

It has become clear that however much we may value the forms of worship to which we have become accustomed, they are totally inappropriate to those who have no experience of the Christian faith. We have a High Church, Anglo-Catholic background, together with a strong charismatic experience. All our services are Eucharistic. We knew that it would be very difficult to introduce people who had never previously been to church into this kind of worship. Those to whom we are called to carry the gospel have no idea what we are talking about. The language and symbolism is incomprehensible. They know of Jesus only in the vaguest possible way.

However, with a second church, we can maintain our Eucharistic worship at Holy Trinity while reaching out with a totally new evangelistic service at St Paul's. The idea developed from a short service we began during Billy Graham's 1989 Mission to London, which we called 'Sunday Special' and which ran from 11.30 a.m. to 12.30 p.m. following our main Family Communion service. But it suffered from the fact that one could not easily make newcomers welcome, when they were arriving rather tentatively just as the previous congregation was pouring out. It felt second-best. The idea was right, but the location and timing was wrong.

Therefore, when we re-opened St Paul's at the end of October last year, we moved the Sunday Special to 11.00 a.m. to become the principal act of worship at that church. It has been highly successful, with genuine conversions nearly every week.

Choosing the Team

One of the problems in a large congregation is making the avowed intention of 'every-member ministry' into a reality. With a highly mobile congregation, there are many men and women, especially younger men and women, who do not find an opportunity to exercise a valuable ministry. The key positions are already occupied, and everyone appears to be very busy.

Therefore, I was able to choose 25 young men and women, who were deeply committed to Christ and baptised in the Spirit, to join me in the mission to the residential population of our parish. None of them were ministering effectively in Holy Trinity, so they did not leave a vacuum. I have to say that I was appalled by the fact that I could have chosen many more from the unrecognised and untapped resources lying dormant in the church of Holy Trinity.

It seemed clear that I should undertake this mission rather than my colleague. As I had been vicar of the parish for nearly twenty years, it was good for Holy Trinity to have a change, and for St Paul's to know that I valued that part of the parochial mission as highly as our mission to the High Street. We now have a senior priest who is responsible for Holy Trinity, leaving me free to develop the next stage of our work.

Benefits to the Receiving Church

There are three dramatic advantages when you take a team into an empty church. The first is that the members of the team are under no illusion. They are there for the sake of those who do not know the Lord Jesus. They are not there because they like the worship, benefit from the teaching, or enjoy their friendship with others; they are there simply and solely to serve. That attitude is contagious, and others who attend rapidly learn the purpose for which our Lord formed his church.

The second advantage is that you can have a mission service that is quite specifically designed for the needs of the outsider, without being tied to any Anglican form of worship. Everybody understands why it is the way it is. Those who come, who are already confirmed members of the church, are encouraged to move to Holy Trinity where they will be able to continue their Christian life and witness.

Third, local interest is stirred by the re-opening of a church, by the evidence of new life, by seeing people coming and going: new notices, new leaflets, and all the signs of returning vitality and excitement. We shall capitalise on that when we close down for rebuilding and move the Sunday Special service into a school for the duration of the building contract. When we re-open next summer, it will be for a seven-days-a-week programme of mission and outreach.

Reaching the Asian Community

In our team we have six Indians, most of them from the Mar Thoma Syrian Church of South India. This is a great blessing to us, and we are discussing with their bishop and synod the possibility of becoming involved in a Local Ecumenical Project with a shared building in order to facilitate a joint mission to the locality.

The younger people, of Hindu families, who were born here or went to school here, are more open to the gospel. We have had some conversions. But there is still a great deal of pressure from their parents and grandparents. They do not want their children to be baptised because they want to arrange a Hindu wedding. They fear that by becoming a Christian, they will deny their cultural heritage. It is for this reason that the Indian team members are so valuable. Not only do they make visiting Indians feel at home, but they demonstrate that you do not surrender your nationality or culture when you accept Jesus Christ as Lord.

After six months we have established a congregation which now averages about 75; and we expect it to double by the end of the year.

Behind this infant plant lie the resources of Holy Trinity, with nurture groups for new Christians, home Bible groups, and a continuing cycle of intercessory prayer. We are thrilled to see people coming who have never been to church in their lives – some, not even as children – and we are certainly reaching parts of the parish that we could not have touched before. For that we praise God.

II: The St Luke's Grafton Satellite

Robin and Ros Holley

The Background

The Grafton Satellite is the second of two satellite congregations in St Luke's parish, Halliwell, Bolton. Situated in a largely Asian part of the parish, which is itself an Urban Priority Area, the satellite began in September 1987, when nineteen members of St Luke's congregation committed themselves to be active founder members. They were not leaving the parish church; rather, we were starting a third Sunday morning service in another part of the parish, with the aim of being a worshipping community there. For the evening service, the members return to the parish church.

The launch of the satellite was based on four years of preparation by the two of us. During that time, we were involved in winning trust and friendship within the community, so that when we felt it right to have a worshipping congregation within the area, people were already prepared to come and join us. Very early on, we had learnt that we had to win trust before we could share faith.

With three simultaneous services on a Sunday morning, the satellites could only work with lay leadership. Team work is vital. All must have a common commitment to working with those of other

races and to understanding their religions. Training
the team to do this effectively is a large part of our
responsibility. Reaching Asian people means being
willing to spend extended time with individuals and
families. Clergy could not give that, but a team of lay
people can, by concentrating on one or two families
rather than mass evangelism.

Our going freed seats at St Luke's to facilitate
further growth, and increased the church's witness in
a part of the parish with many Muslims and some
Hindus. Nevertheless, the need for our team to be
free from parish responsibilities has sometimes been a
problem in our relationship with the parish church,
which has its own priorities and need of lay help.

Sunday Morning Services

We meet in a Red Cross Centre, normally used as a
day centre for the elderly. Two old houses have been
adapted for this purpose. It provides us with a peaceful
and informal location for our services. We operate with
a fair degree of independence, which demands loyalty
to our vicar. Our services should not clone the parish
church, as we are trying to reach a different kind of
community; but we do need to stay within the theological position and general ethos of the parish church.

From the start we believed it vital to have Asians
in the congregation. A man converted from Hinduism
and an Anglo-Indian lady joined us at the first service,
and we have had an Asian presence at virtually every
service since then.

Our services are fairly lively and informal. We use
any musical talent available, and sing mainly newer
songs with a blend of older hymns. Remembering that
some of our congregation speak English as a second
language, we need to avoid archaic and complicated

vocabulary. We read from the Good News Bible, and avoid 1662 liturgy or hymns that will not be understood. This policy also suits white members of this UPA community, who have a different vocabulary from many church people. Language is of no value if it does not communicate.

Once a month we have a family service, when parents are invited, and this is when the largest number of Asian friends come in. We are only able to have communion about once every eight weeks when our vicar or other clergy can be released. Many of us find missing the communion a significant sacrifice.

Numbers are not huge, although we have been up into the sixties at the best-attended services.

Use of Festivals

Asian people are used to festivals and love to celebrate. They come from pluralistic societies, and expect each religion to appear in public on its own festive occasions. Holding a street carnival based on the 'Make Way' material by Graham Kendrick put us on the map. It was a colourful, lively celebration, and included music, dance, drama, clowns and balloons. We wanted to bring a festive mood to the area, and also to push back Satan's hold. At various points we stopped to pray. This made an impression on the Asian community, and we received a tremendous reception as well as sensing a lifting of the spiritual oppression which pervades the area.

We have also held open-air services, which keep us in the public eye even if they do not produce an immediate result (although the first contact with one Hindu family came through an open-air service). English weather conditions do not encourage us to be out on every occasion, but we find certain festivals draw numbers of Hindus and even Muslims into our services. Our Christmas carol service is usually the best attended; but a surprisingly close second is Mothering Sunday which Asian people seem to relate to very well. Our family service numbers double on those occasions and Asians usually outnumber whites in the congregation.

Work Among Children

The community very much appreciates the interest taken in the welfare of its children. We began with a Christmas party for all the neighbours' children; and a street party for the Royal Wedding gave an opportunity to bring white and ethnic communities together. Outings for children who only ever go out to visit relatives are enjoyed. And as parents began to trust us with their children, they were willing for them to join in our holiday clubs and weekly Bible club. It is easier to get Hindu children along to weekly events, as Muslim children have to go to Mosque school daily at 5.00 p.m. Through the children we get to know the whole family, and are able to visit homes more easily. When the satellite congregation began worshipping together and having regular monthly family services, whole families began to come and continue to do so.

In August 1990 we ran a week-long 'Rainbow Club'. Each afternoon, around 80 children met at the Rainbow Bus Stop, with the Rainbow Bus (a decorated minibus owned by a satellite member) cruising round the area to gather them together. We played games, and finished each two-hour programme with a puppet show including a Rainbow feature; and on the final day, 'How the Rainbow came to be.' Alongside the play, there was a Bible-based evening programme using material from Scripture Union. Children were invited to attend, but no pressure was put on them. We began with 34; by the Friday evening we had collected 100 crowded into our small Red Cross centre. The gospel was presented in a clear, uncompromising way using songs, quizzes, a time to think, and an audio-visual presentation of the story for the day. About 95% of the children attending were from Asian families, and were mainly Muslim. On the final evening we held a barbecue for the entire community, serving Halal burgers and listening to an Indian band playing popular music. About 400 came, white and Asian, Christian and non-Christian, Hindu and Muslim. Future, similar events are planned. We came to see the Rainbow as a sign of God's promise to us for that area.

Working with the Asian Community

As a couple we moved into a house in an Asian area, so very naturally we began by being good neighbours. We spent time just listening. It is important not to think that time is being wasted talking about apparently unimportant things. One may not say anything 'spiritual'; but the presence of Jesus goes with you into each situation. People have commented about the peace that they experience when we have visited, or had them in our home.

Like most churches, we find it a struggle to reach men in the white community; but all those who have come to Christ from the Asian community have been men. Women do come to our services; and we have had more ladies' activities than those for men. Why then this response? There are several likely reasons. Asian men have more freedom than women. Men are the decision makers in their society. Spirituality is a quality for which Asian men have high regard. Accordingly, they observe rituals, pray, and often fast. Religion is important to them. Women are responsible for maintaining ancestral religion within their family. It is they who may well feel they have failed if someone becomes a Christian. For all these reasons, it is important for us to create opportunities to witness to men as well as women and children.

Asian people belong to supportive communities. Often, when we ask people to become Christians, we ask them to leave their community; and then we put nothing in its place. So we are looking at ways of giving general community support. One of our ladies is a solicitor who has been given permission by her firm to provide free legal advice one afternoon each week. She has even learnt some Gujarati to make it possible. We are also exploring the possibilities of starting an advice centre, encouraging a lady doctor to open a ladies' surgery in a Muslim area, and initiating other projects to show the love of Christ within the community. We also meet practical needs as they arise, such as hospital visiting, filling in forms for schools and authorities, and making telephone calls to services such as the Gas Board.

Within two months of starting the Grafton satellite, we were approached by a Hindu family experiencing demonic oppression. We had to learn quickly how to deal with that, and be involved in deliverance ministry. We have had to face spiritual attack on ourselves, our family and friends. For our Asian friends, spiritual powers are a fact of life which have always been near at hand. They are looking for spiritual people who know about prayer and fasting, and are not impressed by convincing arguments and carefully thought-out doctrine alone.

This sort of church planting is not work for those who want quick results. Most Asian people have not even begun to understand us. We see the work as very long-term, some of it even preparing for generations not yet born.

CHAPTER FIVE

Planting in Middle-Class Suburbs

Tim Daykin, St Francis, Valley Park, Hampshire

Suburbia and the middle class represent a context in which the Anglican church is traditionally strong. However, this is by no means universally true and many suburban middle-class communities lie well outside any 'Bible belt' or effective church presence. There is still vast scope for strengthening the church in such areas and church planting is one viable option. Even where there is a strong suburban parish church with a thriving 'Bible belt' type congregation, it is likely that it will only be reaching some 10% of their parish population at the most. Hence if we re-focus our attention onto the 'harvest field' of the unchurched, there are always plenty of situations where church planting may be God's calling for the next phase of growth and evangelism.

This case study is described by Tim Daykin. After a curacy in Farnham, Surrey he was chaplain for five years at King Alfred's College, Winchester, Church of England College of Higher Education with some 120 students. He then responded to a call to move within the Southampton Diocese – specifically to pioneer a church plant into a new private housing area in the suburbs of Southampton. Many of the residents commute into the nearby city.

This plant was conceived as a diocesan initiative. Tim tells the story of how he and his wife Ruth slowly established a new community of faith in this middle-class area. It also illustrates one way that the Church of England can respond to neighbourhoods that do not conform to existing parish boundaries. Because this plant was the initiative of the diocese, there was the will to find a formula for changing the legal framework to respond to the new mission challenge. Tim explains how the device of the 'conventional district' enabled the planting area in the suburb of Valley Park to be formed out of three previous parishes.

Another interesting aspect of this plant is that, although it was born in a non-ecclesiastical building, Tim and the diocese felt it right to move the emerging congregation to a new purpose-build facility at a later stage. This was seen as a creative opportunity for innovation as the planted church developed its identity and ministry at the heart of the community.

The Background

Valley Park is five miles north-east of the centre of Southampton. In 1983 there were just two houses surrounded by open fields and woodland; now there are over 1,700 homes with a population of some 5,000. The houses are all owner-occupied, with a high proportion of young families. The local authority is planning a further 1,800 homes, which would double the population by the early years of the next century. Work is provided in the numerous high-tech industries concentrated in the south and Solent region; in commercial and government agencies; and in local industry. Some travel to Basingstoke and even to London.

It is interesting to reflect on the way in which people describe their community. People speak of living 'on' Valley Park. People do not live 'on' Winchester, or

London, or Southampton, but 'in' them. You do live 'on' the Moon, or Mars. All this points to the sense of community which people have. In our experience, the church can play a major role in transforming the 'on' to an 'in'.

The development straddles two local authority districts and three parishes. The Diocese of Winchester was determined that the ministry of the church should be established in the area, and overcame the boundary problem by establishing a Conventional District, which involved removing (with the consent of the respective incumbents) each of the parts of Valley Park from the three existing parishes, to be one independent single unit. Four years later, this has now become a parish in its own right. Valley Park has thus been part of a diocesan strategy to provide for growing areas. This has been achieved both by enhancing and enlarging existing buildings, and by creating new ones from scratch. In the last five years the diocese has backed five completely new churches, with a further one on the drawing board.

The church plant at Valley Park was achieved by a priest moving into the area, into a house purchased by the diocese. The first task was to get to know the area and to become known in the community. Alongside this, establishing a regular pattern of worship and pastoral care was the priority. Worship began in a small temporary community centre. In fact, this is a pair of bungalows, one of which has no internal walls and serves as a modest hall. Four years later, on 9th June 1991, the congregation moved into a new church right at the centre of the community.

Five Issues

Rather than tell the story of ministry in Valley Park, I will highlight five issues that have arisen to show lessons we have learnt.

1. The Parable of the Sower

At the first service in Valley Park, the reading was the parable of the sower. This proved to be prophetic. There were several very enthusiastic people who were there on day one, but who quickly lost their interest and eventually disappeared. They are probably the kind of people who never question the fact that the Church of England is their church, and for whom regular worship means Christmas, Mothering Sunday, and Harvest: the three major festivals as they see them! Before rushing to condemn this level of commitment, we should remember that these folk are the bedrock of vast numbers of parishes, and represent a pool of goodwill waiting to be tapped. But we should not expect them to become regulars, or to contribute in a leadership role.

A second group, like the seed which grew well but was choked by weeds, seemed to flourish but eventually withered away. Why? People come to a church with their own agendas. Perhaps they have not been in a church for three, five, or even ten years. They feel comfortable to begin with, and want things to stay the same. Nothing stays the same for long, so they begin to retreat.

One should not imagine that new churches do not have traditions. They have lots. If, as in Valley Park, one is drawing on people who have no current or even recent church affiliation, then there are diverse traditions and expectations around. There is not the ghost of one vicar to live with, but of fifty.

I need to mention also the seed that fell into fertile

ground. This is where the real surprises have been. Many have become the core members and lay leaders of the congregation.

2. Lay Leaders

In an established church there is ample opportunity to get to know people well before inviting them to take up some leadership role or responsibility. In a new church this is not the case, and it can be a major problem.

Why do people want to assume leadership roles? To serve God? This may be so; but none of us are quite as pure and uncomplicated as that. There are other reasons as well. Perhaps we seek a position of authority in the church which we lack at work, or in any other social group. Perhaps we long to earn recognition, to feel respected and important. Discerning why someone is offering themselves for leadership is a complex business.

The other side to the coin is: Why do clergy want lay leaders anyway? It is to do with sharing the load, acknowledging that people are better at certain things than we are, and allowing the ministry to belong to the whole people of God. But realistically, how many clergy would support the appointment of a hospital porter as church warden, if the local GP was on offer? Why do clergy choose the lay leaders they do? This is a difficult area, and in a new church one that can produce a lot of anguish and heartache.

3. Knowing the Area

Family services, Sunday Schools, Junior Church, and Baptisms are a major route for contact with the folk who live in this area. Market research is essential. In Valley Park, with a population profile bursting at the seams with young families, we would not have got far with an over-sixties club. Even with a population of

5,000, I have not had one funeral in the last five months.

Families, including dads, do come to church, at least to family services. One of our church wardens offered a useful insight, when he remarked that parents will often do things for their children which they would never do for themselves. This is certainly true of owner-occupied, 'nice', Valley Park.

The overall point is that you have to get to know the community the church is planted into. This means living there and sharing its life. Only a priest who has the time and the openness to walk the streets of his patch will get to know the people and earn their affection, loyalty and respect. This is pastoral evangelism. Before we rush to scrap our parish boundaries we ought to make sure we are not burying our pearls of great price in order to gain another of lesser value.

4. The Church Building

The opportunity for the church in Valley Park to create its own home presented one of the greatest challenges of all during the last four years requiring a lot of planning. This meant in the first place doing some theology about what we mean by 'church'. It was essential that our architect listened to us doing this, and recognised that as his brief. We held three congregational meetings at which we talked about why we had all come to church in the first place, and why we thought other people had not. Only at the third meeting were people invited to comment on what sort of building might be appropriate. Out of this came three statements, which must be one of the shortest architect's briefs on record:

i. The whole building is the church and should enable public worship, private prayer and devotion.

ii. It is anticipated that the church will be the only place of worship serving Valley Park as a district area. The building should serve the needs of regular worship as well as provide a setting to which people will willingly come to celebrate the occasional and special services, such as baptism, weddings and funerals.

iii. It is to be a symbol of God's presence within the community, and as such should balance the distinctiveness which properly belongs to a holy place whilst clearly stating its accessibility and integration within the community. The exterior design and landscaping are important in this respect.

The bottom line was that we wanted a church that the whole community would own as theirs, and not a clubhouse for the regular congregation. We had to trust the architect to go away and do something creative with these ideas. The fact that he had listened enabled him to do that. When he came back with his design, I questioned various things, to which he responded, 'But that is what the congregation said.' Had he only listened to the clergy we would have a very different and much less satisfactory church. We are delighted with the result.

5. Transition
The final issue concerns the transition which occurs over time: the process of institutionalisation. This is inevitable, and can be seen as a positive opportunity to safeguard the essence of the church plant and the original charisma.

For this reason, liturgy, structure and ministry are important, because these are the anchors of institution as well as the safeguards. As time goes on, and more church plants pass from the initial charismatic phase to the institutional phase, this aspect will become increasingly important.

Conclusion

Despite all that has been said, the purpose of the whole venture has not been to plant a church or to replace the familiar fabric of Anglican parish life, but to tell the story, to proclaim the gospel news. In all honesty, getting people to come to church in a place like Valley Park, though difficult, is not the hardest job in the world. Getting people into church is one thing: challenging them to become disciples is much more difficult and much more important.

CHAPTER SIX

Planting From Holy Trinity, Brompton

Major cities, and especially London, present difficult mission challenges and opportunities. To list just a few factors, there is high population density with multi-cultured and multi-ethnic communities, high mobility with cars and public transport and little correlation between the historic parish and modern demographics.

In such circumstances it may be easier to build a very large congregation whose members are spread over a wide area. There are advantages and strengths of churches like Holy Trinity, Brompton with over 1,000 members, in terms of a resource centre giving visibility and impacting on city life. However John Collins and Sandy Millar, the leaders at HTB, were concerned for a number of years that other patterns of growth and mission should develop from this strong base. Not only were the facilities full but they had a concern to share the strength God had given them to revitalise other struggling churches in the capital. They were looking for opportunities to give away members, in church planting teams of such a size that they would be more like a 'transplant'. This model would be impossible in most other towns and cities in England but there are real advantages in starting with 75 to 100 people if you are taking over a big Victor-

ian 'barn' with a giant heating bill – not to mention a re-roofing project!

If there are potential advantages, there are also complications such as the available buildings being threatened with closure and situated in a different parish and even a different diocese! Despite the difficulties, Holy Trinity have persevered and repeated this transplant model three times. Although distinct from most other church planting approaches there are still principles and lessons to be learnt, of wide application. The stories told here relate to the first two HTB plantings and are told from the different perspectives of Peter Selby, the bishop of the diocese into which one of the plants was made; Paul Perkin and John Irvine, the two curates who led the respective ventures; and Sandy Millar who continues to lead the mother church. It is relevant, I believe, that not only has there been a third transplant to re-open St Paul's Onslow Square, but that HTB have also given away a small team to pioneer a co-operative plant with Youth with a Mission in a parish church crypt, serving AIDS sufferers and the many street people of Earls Court.

I: The Experience of a Receiving Diocese

Peter Selby, Bishop of Kingston

My first experience of church planting was in 1973, when I was in the lay training team in the Diocese of Southwark. A new Canon Missioner was appointed, Ivor Smith Cameron, who insisted that there would be a Sunday congregation in his house. That had to be negotiated; and in a way things have turned full circle, as we later negotiated for him to bring that congregation from a house in Clapham to another house in Battersea, which happens also to be a parish church. In a curious way he has moved from planting in one setting to something much more conventional. I was also involved when St Luke's Norwood undertook a plant within their parish, which was straightforward from my perspective.

My third experience of church planting is the subject of this chapter, the move of a group from Holy Trinity Brompton to a parish in Battersea: St Mark's Battersea Rise. It was a long process, but with two distinct phases. The first was an approach by the staff at Holy Trinity Brompton to see whether there would be a church, destined for redundancy, that would be convenient for their many existing members who lived in South Battersea. I met with both the staff of Holy Trinity, and with a group of the lay people there who lived in South Battersea.

Many of these people had been students or young professional single people, who had come to faith at Holy Trinity. As they began to establish themselves, they had found that buying or renting property in Chelsea was prohibitively expensive, and many moved to Battersea instead. So the situation was originally caused by something as mundane and secular as the housing market.

At the time of this original approach, I did have some discussions within the deanery, and it was quite clear that the project would not be acceptable. The possibility of a chapel being established within somebody else's parish and without parochial responsibilities was not welcomed, and people said all the standard things some of which were very harsh and hurtful. I did not expect to hear about the matter again. However, at a later date when we had two vacant parishes in South Battersea, I received a letter from Holy Trinity, saying: 'We have heard that these two vacancies have occurred – is there any chance that either of them might be the place where we could plant a congregation?'

Once again, I started discussions around the deanery and with the Bishop of Southwark. There was a problem, in that we had four churches in South Battersea, but the diocesan plan only allowed for three incumbents: if we replaced all the people, the planned staff reduction would not be achieved. But as soon as I began to discuss the proposal with various people, the atmosphere was entirely different. There was a strong feeling in the deanery (with one or two exceptions) that if the plan was for someone to come with a congregation to work a parish, then that was entirely different from the previous proposal, and people were very happy for it to happen.

There were exceptions, and I suppose because the sense of threat was strongest, it was the evangelical churches who found this most difficult and who felt they were likely to lose membership.

We have a system in the Diocese of Southwark that the bishop has ten discretionary places, which are used for compassionate appointments where people are ill and need lighter work, and also for missionary experiments. I asked for one of these places for this project, and it was agreed. In October 1987, Paul Perkin was appointed as Priest in Charge of the Parish of St Mark, Battersea Rise, and came with quite a large group.

I want to offer a few reflections on this process. The first is that bishops are human. Like all human beings, when confronted with a choice between life and death, they have a tendency to choose death because it is less problematic! This is particularly true on a bad day. Contrary to what people believe, bishops get tired and fractious; and some of the things that go wrong with church planting are not mysterious, but happen because human beings are dealing with human beings.

The second reflection is that negotiating a church plant is like any other kind of negotiation: the negotiations succeed when everybody wins. So identifying that win/win possibility is a key aspect. In the case of St Mark's Battersea Rise, I am full of gratitude to Paul, to the congregation, and to God, for transforming a desperate situation.

Third, there is a great deal of caricaturing on both sides. It is not a very good opening gambit, to say to a bishop: 'I know that you are concerned about parish boundaries, but we are concerned about winning people for Christ.' The bishop is sitting there thinking: 'Oh. I thought I was interested in that also.' Of course there are caricatures the other way, like the tiny established congregation who say to the new one: 'You are a group of like-minded people; we serve the whole parish', said by a church that has done nothing except freeze people out whenever they have appeared.

My last reflection is this: never imagine that the issue is settled. There is always a possibility that the plant will plant again, that new and exciting possibilities will open up after one has been embraced. There are other kinds of issue that are never settled, things to do with the history and tradition of particular parishes. Paul and I are still struggling with things that have to do with the place they took on. It is very important to retain a close relationship with diocesan authorities once things have been negotiated, because new, unexpected things will always come up. A close, continuing, supportive relationship is essential.

II: Negotiations from the Planter's Perspective

Paul Perkin, Priest in Charge, St Mark's Battersea Rise

The whole experiment of planting the church in South Battersea has been a tremendously happy and fruitful one. Even so, there have been pressure points, and I will identify four of these.

One pressure point was the initial, mutual suspicion between ourselves and the diocese. Because this plant was across not just a parish or even a deanery boundary, but across a diocesan boundary, there was no relationship to build on before the plant took place. And there was a background of comments made to the bishop like: 'Let that lot get their foot in the door and you will never hear the last of them'. On our side there was an impression of a reluctant bureaucracy dragging its heels over months and years.

Our initial meetings tended to be formal, thrashing out issues of tension, in the knowledge of strong feelings in the background (for example, from other local clergy in that area). I was only introduced into the process at the very final stage before the plant took place. The previous discussions had taken place between the vicar of Holy Trinity and the Diocese of Southwark.

The second pressure point was a personal one. By

the time I was brought into the negotiations, the expectation and hope was that one meeting with the bishop and archdeacon would iron out all the remaining problems. I would then be invited to go ahead with the plant. But although there was a tremendous signal from Holy Trinity that they wanted to plant in Battersea, I still needed convincing of my own involvement at that point. I should have asked far more questions and talked about the support I needed. Instead, the tone was one-sided: 'If we are going to let you go ahead and do this, there are certain conditions.'

Third, there was the matter of continuity between the old ministry of St Mark's and the new one. One priority was the welfare of the remnant of the old congregation, which was five or ten, mainly elderly, ladies. Another matter was the continuation of various activities related to the old ministry, but which had become so detached from the church that they were outside the church's sphere of influence. For example, there was a workshop for four or five disabled people using the main ministry premises of the church, apart from the worship area.

As things turned out, the welfare of the remnant was no problem at all. Most stayed and have been a tremendous asset in the ministry since. But over other aspects of continuity, there was a divergence of views between myself and the diocese. We were actually helped by the fact that the derelict church building was falling down. The work we had to put in hand on the building bound us together with a sense of common mission.

I had learnt to relate to the London diocese, which has its particular theological persuasion. Southwark has a very different emphasis, and this transition required a very steep learning curve for me. Normally, a vicar goes to a church intending to get into the parish slowly, making no sudden changes for a year or two, and then gradually putting the stamp of his own ministry on the church. There is time for the congregation to adjust, and for the diocese to get used to him. But in the case of a church plant, the expectations of the planting group are for immediate change. The situation was made more complex by divergence over immediate issues of pastoral practice, theological emphasis, and moral and ethical matters.

The fourth pressure point is again personal. I became a church planter and an incumbent at the same moment; and I had no training for either. I can see that some of the early difficulties were a result of the tensions of being on my own in a very new and strange world. I hope that some work will now be done to help people to combine becoming leader of a church and taking a church plant simultaneously.

III: Planting St Barnabas, Kensington

John Irvine, St Barnabas, Kensington

The Story of St Barnabas

St Barnabas was also a transplanted church from Holy Trinity. It began with the vicar, John Collins, praying in his study in the vicarage. I had joined John as a curate in 1981, and was there for four years, during which time the church grew to about 1,300. The church was naturally thinking about transplanting, or church planting.

The most obvious geographical area to plant or transplant into was south of the Thames, in Clapham or Wandsworth which were both still in the London Diocese. That was where a large number of people who had been converted and trained at Holy Trinity had moved, as they had married and started families. They had maintained their church allegiance there, and formed quite a large gathering. So we made enquiries, explored, and saw the bishop, but nothing transpired at that time. It was not until later that Holy Trinity successfully transplanted to St Mark's Battersea Rise.

We were all concerned to ensure planting within the system. We had a commitment to the Anglican church, and felt that God had called us to work there. Transplants and church planting generally are part of God's plan for the Church of England. So we resisted the temptation to do something on our own, and looked for an opportunity to do something within the structure. The diocese was aware of our thinking, and in the end Mark Santer, then Bishop of Kensington, asked John Collins and myself whether we would be interested in taking on St Barnabas. This is about three miles from Holy Trinity, across both parish and deanery boundaries.

Mark was perfectly open about the reason for this. St Barnabas was a huge Victorian barn which had fallen on sad times. It was built to seat over 1,000 people, but the congregation had dwindled to under 20. There was a serious problem with the roof, and there was no heating. Nobody with any sense would look at it.

It seems to me, that with the model of transplants within the system, this is just the sort of thing we should be looking for. For the diocese, it was a white elephant which needed resources and people, which we were willing to give. We did not ask for any funds from the diocese. The quota had not been paid for some time, so we asked not to be saddled with past debts; but otherwise we said we would take it on, although there was an estimated £250,000 roof repair in prospect.

We shared the project with the Holy Trinity Congregation, and prayed for quite a large number to commit themselves to go. It seemed right to plant in strength, because of the magnitude of the task in this instance. Prayers were answered, and in 1985 we set off with just over 100 people. Of the original congregation at St Barnabas, only three left, which was encouraging. Three of the others were still on the PCC. The original congregation, which I had thought was 'dead', had actually been praying just as we had been, and one of the things I had to ask forgiveness for was my arro-

gance. After two years I asked one of them how they
had coped with all the change. The reply was, 'We
stayed through death, and stuck here when others
were leaving, so we weren't going to leave when life
came.'

The early days were an extraordinary and exciting
adventure, with a great deal happening very quickly.
There was much cleaning and painting, a new heating
system, new toilets and carpet. God's people gave gen-
erously in time, energy and money.

We have grown, God has blessed us, and numbers
have increased to around 800. We now have a staff of
nine, and are looking for new opportunities, again
within the system. We are considering multiple congregations and services, but our vision is to give of our
best again, to a semi-redundant church, and to send
off a curate with a number of people.

Principles and Practice

Planting begins with vision. John Collins began by
talking about church planting, going to conferences,
getting excited about it. The excitement was contagious, and infected many of the people in the large
church of Holy Trinity, who had been blessed and built
up but were longing for a new adventure and a new
stage of service.

Having got the vision, the next thing is getting the
support. The bishop's support is vital, especially where
crossing parish boundaries, or receiving a new parish,
is the proposal. He needs to be persuaded about the
opportunities and the possibilities, and the advantages
for the diocese. The support of nearby clergy matters
as well. I had not realised that planting and transplanting could be threatening. I wish now that I had
spent more time going to local clergy, and explaining

what we were trying to do. We have recovered to some extent, and now have good relations. We are very committed to the chapter, and to playing our part in the deanery synod. But there is still an understandable fear and concern among local clergy.

It is wise to be involved in the strategic committees in the diocese. Church planters and pioneers often are not very good at working with the system. In our diocese, we have identified three committees: the pastoral committee which oversees various pastoral organisations; the redundant churches committee; and the finance committee. These seem to be the key committees, in terms of opportunities to cross boundaries. Because we are involved, we know when redundant or semi-redundant churches are coming up; we know which churches are struggling; we know about pastoral reorganisation plans; and we have every chance to come in and say, 'What about this as a possibility?' We have tried with one particular church building, and this did not actually come to anything, but it was much easier to discuss because of time spent in building up relationships.

The next step is getting the people to form the team. There are many different ways to approach this. One way is to ask all those living in the area of the plant to go. Another might be to ask particular home groups to go. We considered this, but reflected that there might be people in a particular home group or postal district who still needed for some reason or other to belong to the mother church. So we decided simply to let those people come who wanted to come. This meant in practice that the group which formed was already in pastoral relationship. One or two came for geographic or other reasons; but for most it was because of some relationship with others in the group. This proved to be a tremendous benefit.

For us, it was right to plant in strength. I would not

suggest it must normally be as many as 100, but the underlying principle is to give the best. Holy Trinity found it painful to see some of their trusted leaders go out, but God has made up to them that painful loss. Certainly, from the receiving end, it was wonderful to have the many gifts of those in the team.

Commitment is important, and we asked people to sign up for a year. The reasoning behind that was that after a week or two, if the sense of adventure was waning and people began to remember the warmth and numbers in the mother church, it would be tempting for some to return. This would undermine confidence. Sometimes we had disastrous Sundays, when there was no heating and nothing seemed to work. It would have been a great stress on the leaders, to be thinking: 'Will anyone turn up next week?'

Joys and Problems

Among the joys are adventure and growth, building on existing relationships, and the support and help of the sending church. There are some problems to mention as well. The ecclesiastical structure is not designed to cope with church plants across boundaries, and it is well to realise that there will be difficulties. Faculties, for example: often a transplant will move into a building that requires a lot of investment quickly. I rushed ahead knocking holes in walls everywhere, and asking for decisions quickly, and that caused a lot of trouble.

The most painful difficulty was the misunderstanding of motives by fellow clergy. I do not know to what extent that was due to the numbers involved, or because of my bad handling of it, or because of the reputation of Holy Trinity. But the suspicion of other churches was very hard.

Another problem is getting transfer growth rather than conversion growth. The purpose of transplants and going across boundaries is to win more for God's kingdom; but a new church will always attract disaffected people from other churches, people who want a change. One has to be aware of that, and resist the false impression that everything is going well, when there is just transfer growth. I do not mean to imply that in our case the growth was all transfer growth. Among the 100 initial congregation were a lot of gifted evangelists, and that has been a factor for us.

Undoubtedly, the joys far outweigh the problems. I am very happy where I am, and see it as a lifetime ministry – although at the moment I am still priest-in-charge. The only thing that might persuade me to leave would be the opportunity to plant again. I do not think anything quite compares with the joy and excitement of those first few years.

IV: The Perspective of the Sending Church

Sandy Millar, Holy Trinity, Brompton

My purpose is to identify what will be helpful for any church contemplating starting a plant.

A Theology of Planting

The first need is for a theology of planting. If people have no understanding of why they are doing something, they will soon get immensely discouraged. A commitment through teaching, example or discussion is needed, to put the topic on the agenda for every group in the church. The 'theology for planting' would include a concept of how many unconverted people there are, what the gospel is, and what the great commission is.

One can offer helpful pictures. Commercial firms know that the more check-outs they have, the more people they can process; so that is one picture. Another picture is that of the family, with a natural stage of family life being about having children. At some point, the children move off and the family moves into a grandparent stage of encouragement and support.

This picture has been especially true for us, as we have only ever planted with a member of staff into an Anglican church. First, there was St Barnabas Church with John Irvine; and then St Mark's Battersea Rise with Paul Perkin; and now we have launched St Paul's Onslow Square, which is in the parish. Each time the plant has to be set up like a new family in a new home from the mother church. The attitude towards them depends a lot on our theology, and if people have an understanding of that then it is all easier to accept.

Models of Planting

The second need is for a model. After our first experience with St Barnabas we were much better equipped and prepared. When we first went to see the Bishop of Kingston about a possible plant into St Mark's, the archdeacon advised us not to talk about 'church planting' and not to use the expression; that language was not used outside certain circles. Now it is much more widely used, which is very helpful: there are more models available.

Facing the Cost

The third need is for getting beyond the theology and the models and actually taking the plunge and doing it in practice. This is costly. It is costly in leadership, because the ones that want to go and start are the keen ones, the ones you had based future hopes and plans upon. They are the people who were going to run all the home groups, the sort who respond straight away to what the church is offering. The church has to remember that they all belong to the Lord, and to be able to let them go.

It is also costly in money, because these keen people are the ones who are covenanting. I remember when my entire mail for a year seemed to be requests to transfer covenants to St Mark's Battersea Rise!

Misunderstanding

A further cost is in misunderstanding. With Battersea, a lot of people felt that our object was to build an empire. This 'empire' has cost the church £120,000 a year; it has cost all our best leaders who the church has nurtured; and in fact is no empire at all, because the new churches are totally independent, operating in their own deaneries or dioceses.

Rebuilding

Finally, there is the cost of rebuilding afterwards. We suddenly find that we have lost a lot of people: they have the excitement, we have the sense of loss. The only saving grace is that we can refer to our theology, and rejoice in the fact that if St Mark's, St Barnabas, and St Paul's all got together they would not fit in the building of Holy Trinity. That carries us through. In fact, we have to find new ways of doing it, because we are all committed to the excitement of church planting.

CHAPTER SEVEN

Planting in a Newcastle Urban Priority Area

Tony Adamson

We now move to the extreme North East and a project in a particularly deprived Urban Priority Area (UPA). The story typifies many of the needs of these areas in our major cities – highlighted by the Faith in the City *report. It also ends by asking uncomfortable questions about the longer term future – even in cases like this one at Benwell, where the church has seen substantial growth and development of ministry.*

An encouraging aspect of this plant is the creative ways that partnership and shared responsibility have facilitated this work. It all started over a decade ago with a town centre parish in Jesmond where Tony Adamson was a lay member of the congregation. David Holloway was vicar of this strong church and he shared his vision for church planting with Tony. One of his suggestions was for his parish to help finance such pioneer projects into unchurched UPA neighbourhoods. After his training and ordination Tony first went as curate to the parish of St Paul's Elswick. He stayed there for five years and learnt much about urban ministry in that time. It was during this period that the next-door estate of Benwell was identified as almost completely unchurched. Although David Holloway was ready to help finance a worker there, when Tony was appointed curate, this was not needed. However, David and the Jesmond parish (which is in the same diocese but not the same deanery as Benwell) continued to seek ways to support the venture. Later they helped finance a co-worker for Tony. They contributed part of the stipend for a Church Army evangelist, Scott MacDonald, who moved into Benwell.

In this chapter Tony tells the story with continuing examples of co-operation. Members of the neighbouring Anglican and Methodist churches play supporting roles at key stages of the development – from encouragement at the first carol service to providing a staff member for the drop-in shop project. This is not the only plant to be facilitated by such partnering initiatives where churches that have resources to share with a UPA. Again this is a pattern suggested in the Faith in the City *report.*

Church planting is certainly not glamorous as these stories show. It requires great perseverance through discouragement and periods of little fruitfulness. However, its pioneer quality and exciting opportunities to reach the totally unchurched are both rewarding and gripping. Scott MacDonald moved on from Benwell in the spring of 1991 and looked for another pioneer challenge. He has moved to an area of West Belfast which is relatively unchurched and hopes to see some re-planting there. Anne and Roger Dyer (Chapter 11) have commented that their experience of the tears and joys of church planting in Chatham had 'ruined' them for any other ministry – they would not want to settle for anything other than the pioneering challenge of church planting.

The Background

Old South Benwell consisted of long rows of terraced houses. In the fifties and sixties, the area came to be regarded as slum housing, and the properties were demolished around 1970. Employment prospects were decreasing. In the seventies, new estates were built and looked very nice: they had central heating and

inside toilets, and were generally regarded as a big
improvement. However, many of the old problems of
urban malaise continued: high unemployment, many
single-parent families, vandalism, crime, prostitution
and alcoholism. Health problems were much higher
than in other parts of Newcastle.

There are three estates in South Benwell. The
Rachel Maughan Estate is the nicer of the two council
estates, and most people there have a job and no desire
to move. The Buddle Road estate is the so called 'problem estate', which attracts headlines in the *Evening
Chronicle* like 'Residents Escape Estate of Fear'. It has
a prison-block feel to it. Lastly, the Guinness Trust
Estate is owned by a housing association and employs
three caretakers who pick up the rubbish and cut the
grass. This is the nicest of the three estates.

People who live in the area consider crime to be the
major problem. Every house in South Benwell has a
one-in-six chance of being burgled in any given year.
These are just reported burglaries: many more are
never reported, since people rarely have insurance. A
local crime prevention initiative has been set up by
the police to try to combat this. Vandalism is very
common, and everyone complains about the appear-
ance of the area, and the way things are wrecked and
spoilt. The result is a general apathy. People just can't
be bothered to look after things any more, because
they feel they are going to be destroyed or stolen.
Often, as you walk around the streets of South
Benwell, you will see the odd armchair or supermarket
trolley lying in the road, as people stop taking responsibility for their community.

This in turn leads to many empty houses. All those
people with any social ambition – a bit of get-up-and-
go – have gone. If you have a job, if you want to
improve your standard of life or the quality of life of
your children, you move off the estate. The only people

who move in are those who are desperate for a house, and people who have other kinds of problems; people just out of prison, alcoholics and people who find it hard to manage. There is a spiralling downwards effect.

David Sheppard, the Bishop of Liverpool, calls this kind of community 'the community of the left behind.'

The church has left too, in many ways. The old Methodist church is now a snooker hall. The old Baptist church is now a community centre. Two Anglican churches have been pulled down. The other Baptist church is run down and neglected. Jesus may certainly be relevant to the present day; but in South Benwell the perception is that the church has retreated and failed.

At the top of the hill from South Benwell is the parish church of St James. There, you can go through the iron gates and the big wooden doors, step into a very large church, take your place in their firm wooden pews, and be handed the *Alternative Service Book 1980* with 1,000 pages of tightly-worded print. This church is some distance geographically from the people of South Benwell, but a great deal further away culturally.

St James is in the main Benwell shopping area. It is within a team ministry with two small churches, St John's and The Venerable Bede; however, all three churches are in the northern part of the parish, away from the Benwell estates. Close to St James is the Bond Methodist Church. In April 1986 I was appointed curate in the team ministry, with responsibility for St John's. Because of the small size of St John's, it has been possible for me to commit myself to the work in South Benwell.

Eight Principles for Action

There are eight principles with which I have worked in the area. The first of these is that you have to live there. People are surprised to find a clergyman and his wife living in the area, instead of in a big vicarage somewhere, but it is important. Our children go to the same school, and I see the other parents in the mornings when I am walking along there. The purpose is to try and identify with the local community as far as is possible, to be one of them.

The second principle is that two are better than one. I was grateful to Scott MacDonald, a Church Army captain who joined me shortly after I moved in. Sometimes we want the church to spread resources as thinly as possible, to try and cover the ground, but that is a very defensive strategy. To use a military analogy, you spread your defences across a wide area to cover all possible areas of attack, but when you go on the offensive, you mass your resources together and punch a hole through the enemy lines. In our urban areas, the church needs to go on the attack.

Listening is the third principle. We did not go in with any set ideas of what would happen, but with a broad brief to evangelise. We spent lots of time just talking to people and trying to find out the sort of things they wanted. We also listen to God and spend much time in prayer, individually and together, and praying around the streets of the area, seeking God's way and not trying to impose our pattern.

Fourth, we developed a strategy of working on institutions first, then individuals, and finally on some kind of service of worship to which we could attract people. For example, I became a governor at the local primary school, and I used to take occasional assemblies. Schools always welcome clergy interest. It was also easy to meet the young people in the youth club.

I would go into Buddle Road Youth Club – it looks like Fort Knox, because it is always getting broken into, and its disco equipment stolen – and talk to the youth club leaders and the youngsters, just to make myself known.

Another group are the elderly in the community centres and old people's clubs. I would go in, have lunch with them, and play cards and bingo. One feature of the area is the low take-up of some of the services offered. There must have been 100 pensioners who could have used the luncheon club, but I found just half a dozen: again, a symptom of the apathy, loneliness, and unwillingness to join things.

Next, we decided to do some door-to-door visiting. I hate this, as it makes me feel like a Jehovah's Witness, but we wanted to let people know we were around. So we did our door-to-door visiting, and then as it was getting near to Christmas we had a carol service in the local community room. We invited a crowd from St James, to make sure that it would be full, that was the first service we ever had after about nine months there.

A fifth principle is the use of house groups. We find these very important. We got contacts from the institutions and clubs, from the door-to-door work, and from the carol service. From these we were able to form some informal house groups. These did not have a set time of meeting, but people drifted in and drifted out. They did not have a set Bible study subject, but it was more a case of people meeting for an evening, and having a gossip with some Christian input from the leader. They were very informal and small, groups of about three or four people willing to get together. After those groups had been meeting for a few months, some fizzled out, others carried on, and they began to say, 'Well, when are we going to have this new church that you have been talking about?'

Therefore, after twelve months in the area, we were able to introduce regular Sunday afternoon worship in one of the local community centres.

The sixth principle we worked to was that the worship should be culturally appropriate. Our worship style is very different from traditional Anglicanism. It is non-liturgical, it is very informal and free flowing. Many of our attenders either cannot read, or struggle with reading. When I conduct a service, it is not so much like a preacher in his pulpit or a priest at his altar, but more like a night club comic, in the style of banter and rapport that develops between me and the congregation.

It was not all that difficult to get together a small worshipping group. However, we are Anglican, and have a responsibility to the whole parish. We wanted to do something to meet the needs of the whole area. People do still live in community there, and there is not the individualisation of a suburban estate. People do know their neighbours, even if they do not like them and can hear them arguing through the walls. From this came our seventh principle: meeting community needs.

During our door-to-door visiting, we had taken round a questionnaire which asked people various things about the area. Unemployment was mentioned, but we did not feel we could do anything about that at the time. But local facilities were also mentioned, and there we felt there was something we could do.

A group of people from St James, together with a group from Bond Methodist, had been considering opening a coffee shop at the top of the hill, where all the rest of the shops are. The group then changed their plans, and decided it would be better placed in the area of greatest need. They got in touch with me, and found a property in Buddle Close, an old shop that the council could not let because nobody wanted it.

A lot of vandalism had taken place and it was a tremendous mess, but with a lot of volunteer help from St James and the Methodist church, it was transformed. It became the Cornerstone Christian Shop, and was opened in September 1987. We got a local TV personality, himself originally from Benwell, to come and open it.

The shop consists principally of a cafe that serves light snacks, coffee and sandwiches. There is also a room with second-hand clothes and books. A small room is available for counselling – or perhaps that is too fancy a word – for private interviews when people come in with forms from the DHSS, or from the Council, or from the Gas Board, which they are having problems filling in. Or perhaps there are other difficulties which they need to talk about privately.

An office is open from around 10.00 a.m. to 4.00 p.m. on weekdays, originally manned by Scott MacDonald, who had experience of shop management. As Cornerstone has developed, it now has two full-time staff, both lay people. One was a member of St James with a long involvement with the area; and the other is an Assistant Manager, a previously unemployed local man from the estate. He gives the shop a credibility that it might not otherwise have. The appointment was enabled by a grant from the Church Urban Fund. So we have done something in a limited way about local unemployment.

In Newcastle, certain wards are designated Urban Priority Areas, and these areas have a Local Priority Area Team, consisting of elected councillors together with an appointed team leader. Our Local Priority Area Team has helped us in various ways, and for the shop they provided a computer and word processor. This has helped Cornerstone to host a Credit Union, a kind of cooperative bank which assists people to save, and tries to keep them out of the hands of the

loan companies and loan sharks who lend in some
cases at extortionate rates of interest. The Local
Authority helped us to set this up.

There is also a larger room, a lounge which we used
for the early meetings of our local church, for prayer
groups, and for occasional meetings. Other groups on
the estate, such as the local Tenants' Association, use
it as well.

A community architect involved with refurbishing
the estate came and met the local people here. Many of
the houses are now being removed, with whole blocks
demolished, and the estate is being improved in con-
junction with local tenants' groups. The Cornerstone
is the focus of much of that activity. So although large
areas of the estate are still derelict, the hope is that
there will be some major improvements, and there is
a sense among residents that things are going to get
better.

The main thrust of the Cornerstone is as a place for
local people to meet. It very quickly became the centre
for local activity, because there is so little else going
on. We were surprised how many people used the
place. Local families come in and sit there all day with
their cups of tea, getting to know one another and
creating a sense of community. Many single men use
the place too. It saves their own heating bills if they
come and sit here, old and young. Many people say
that this project has revolutionised the estate, and
become a sign of hope amidst all the gloom. Cornerstone is to be extended shortly, with neighbouring flats
being made available at low cost by the council.

Our final principle is to try to make the project
and the church indigenous, to make it less reliant on
incomers like myself or like the folk from the nearby
churches. As our local church has grown, it has moved
to a larger community centre, and now to a church
that was abandoned by an independent group. Many

of the services are lay-led. House groups have continued as well. These are also lay-led, and people get
most of their teaching and understanding of the
Christian faith from them rather than from the
Sunday service, which is more of a celebration event.

But we have only scratched the surface. There are
still hundreds and hundreds of families who are never
touched by the church, and that causes me to ask
radical questions about the whole future of the church
and its style in urban areas. We are there: but can we
survive?

CHAPTER EIGHT

Mobilising the Laity in Bolton

Patricia Wick

*We have already observed that church planting involves
mobilising all sorts of new lay ministry. Many church plants
are entirely lay-led. One of the significant contributions of
recent church planting has been the extending of lay ministry
and leadership categories.*

*Pat Wick shares her experience of training and mobilising
the laity in a planting team that established a congregation
in a bowling club. She was perhaps especially well prepared
for her role having been used in that same parish of St Luke's
Bolton in lay leadership and ministry herself from 1981 to
1984 before her theological training and ordination. She
later returned in 1986, and in the church planting model
used at St Luke's, Pat was released to give most of her time
to train, encourage and supervise the lay teams. In many
other cases assistant clergy are also taking this role in church
plants. However some plant teams are made up entirely of
lay people; in such cases these same principles may need to
be applied partly by the clergy at the mother church before
planting and partly by the lay leaders themselves.*

There are tremendous benefits in being allowed to
minister as a lay person, as I know from my own

experience as a lay assistant for three years at Bolton. After that I went to Oak Hill theological college to train for ordination. The way opened up for me to go back to the same church in Bolton, just when they were discussing church planting because the parish church could not hold the people who wanted to come on Sunday mornings (despite twice extending a fairly new church). God was saying to us, 'Stop building walls, and start building bridges into the parish.'

The parish is small, about 4,500 people a mile and a half from the centre of Bolton. I took a nucleus of around 30 people, to plant a satellite church meeting in a bowling club just 300 yards from the parish church. A year later, we took a further group of 20 people to start a second satellite meeting at the Red Cross centre at the Asian end of the parish, which has been described in chapter 4.

One of my aims in ministry has always been to do myself out of a job. I remember hearing a man in his late sixties say, 'I am doing things now that I never dreamt I would be doing four years ago.' We found that the parish church was actually full of very gifted lay people, but because there were so many there, they had been stifled in their ministry. What they needed to do was to discover what their gifts were, and to be set free to use those gifts. Planting out satellite churches was a way of doing that.

The method we used when looking for a team of people to start a satellite church was to put the challenge to the PCC and to the congregation as a whole. Out of that, people came forward and said that God was calling them to be involved. We felt that element was very important: people should be called, not just go because they think the worship might be free, or that things might happen in the satellite churches which could not happen in the parish church. We asked for an initial commitment of a year. That way, whether it was tough or easy, we knew we could stick together.

There was a cost involved in leaving the parish church. People felt at home there, and the standard of what was done was high. However, the planters could still worship at the evening service, and be involved during the week. The two satellites are very much under the wing of the mother church.

One thing we discovered was that people would rarely volunteer when needs were expressed from the front of the church. We needed to consider the members of the church, and try to identify the potential and the gifts which they had. We would then suggest to them that they had these gifts. We found it was very important to teach about the role of lay people from the pulpit as well, and to point out that the satellites would find it difficult to function without lay people being involved. In the end, one of the main benefits of church planting in our church was not the growth of numbers, but the development of people's individual ministries.

My aim as I took lay people into the satellite was to discover their gifts, and set them free to use them. Some of these people had very low self-esteem, and needed to be told what their worth was in the eyes of God. We tried to use the less obvious people, not the ones who were already overloaded with jobs in the life of the church.

Once the gifts were discovered, training was needed. My strategy was to train by experience, because when people try things, they discover whether or not they can do them well. So to some extent, they were thrown in at the deep end. But I would get them to work alongside me on a one-to-one basis: take them out visiting, or sit with them as they prepared a talk, or show them how I would prepare a sermon. It meant spending time with each person in what they were doing.

We also used the conferences that were available. We sometimes felt that the diocesan conferences were not the most helpful ones for our particular needs. So we produced some of our own training courses, for door-to-door work and for Sunday school work, preaching etc.

Assessment was an important part of the process. Sometimes, when someone started leading a service or preaching a sermon, one would realise that actually it was not what they should be doing. That needed to be handled carefully, and people had to accept that as part of the process of discovering gifts. By contrast, sometimes it is right to leave people to get on with what they are doing on their own. One of the satellites in the Asian end of the parish has more or less looked after itself, and we have seen people emerging and taking an initiative there.

We wanted to enable people to serve in a very wide area of ministry, whether it was liturgically at the front, or in music, or in visiting, or children's work, or planning the services. In the satellites, we found we could take risks. Sometimes, someone who one would not dare to ask to read a lesson in the parish church could do it in a satellite, and if they failed then people would love them for it. The fact that some did fail would encourage others to have a go. Allowing people to fail is important.

Some of the people we used were quite inexperienced. When we started the first satellite, we were looking for an organist. We found a young man who had only just started coming to church. He was very good at the organ, but he was not a Christian. Should we use his gifts? We did in fact ask him to play for us, and within about six weeks he became a Christian, followed by four members of his family.

Problem Areas

We found that leadership was important in releasing
and using lay people within the satellites. At one stage
we tried a system whereby five leaders led the congregation between them. That did not work: the congregation was unable to look to five different people as
leader. One overall leader was needed.

There is a problem with clergy versus laity. Some
people are only happy to be visited by clergy: if they
do not see the dog-collar, they will not accept the visit.
Some are hesitant about lay people preaching. There
was a learning process, and once people began to benefit from the wide variety of lay ministry, it was
accepted. Of course, there were problems with personalities and relationships, which took a great deal
of time to sort out. Limitations on Holy Communion
proved difficult, as celebrating this meant bringing the
vicar from the parish church.

Lay people need a lot of support. People are under
great pressures in their homes and in their jobs. The
pastoral care of those in the satellite leadership positions was vital, so that people did not get missed out.
Another lesson we learnt was that expectations must
be realistic. Growth in the satellites was not as fast
as we expected, and we tended to focus on the numbers
that came each week. We had to learn that the most
important aspect was not how many were there, but
what God was doing.

There is also the problem of oneself as a leader,
coping with being surrounded by lay people doing
things. I had to let go, to delegate, and that was sometimes difficult, especially when some lay people may
actually be doing things better than the clergy! Sometimes, the jobs that one is best at, or enjoys most, are
the ones that are being handed over. There is a need

to sit back, even allowing people to do things less well than you would have done yourself.

It is a matter of being open and sharing oneself. The training and equipping of lay people can actually remove you from the front-line work that you were first called to do. But there are tremendous benefits as well. I often felt that lay people complemented me, and covered my weaknesses. They are a great source of encouragement, imagination and ideas. When we were considering how to bring more young mothers to the church, one lady suggested that we walk down the back streets and see where the nappies were hanging on the line. So we went out looking for nappies! It is the lay people that have actually lived longest in the area: as an outsider, I did not really understand the needs of the people in that area of Bolton, but the lay people did.

The time came when the Bishop of Manchester told me I had been in the parish long enough and should move on, so that threw up the problem of changing leadership. I had teams of lay people in the satellites, so I was gradually withdrawing myself anyway. But in my absence, the vicar is having to take on more work in the oversight and coordination of the satellites. We have not been allowed another stipendiary member of staff. What has actually happened is that the church has taken a step of faith and decided to appoint two new workers. Recently a full-time community worker and a full-time youth worker have been employed, to be paid for by the parish church itself.

I am all in favour of lay leadership, but we need to handle it well. We need to discover people's gifts, to train them, to set them free, and at the same time to be aware of the dangers. Let us rejoice that we are all different, have different ministries, and can be enabled to use them.

CHAPTER NINE

New Life in a Redundant Church

Bruce Collins, Notting Hill Gate

We have seen how a very large church like Holy Trinity Brompton can draw on its great strength of resources and transplant into near-redundant buildings and even re-open a closed one. However, much church life in our capital city is on a much smaller scale; this story illustrates that this need not be a barrier to similar exciting adventures of faith. Here a congregation of not much over 100 was the launching pad for a small team which not only re-opened a very large building, but transformed it into a versatile community facility.

This is another example of a plant originating from a non-evangelical parish: the tradition of the mother church was traditional catholic. However, a lovely aspect of the work of God in this case was how Bruce Collins, the curate who took on the planting team, although from a different tradition, learnt so much more from the interaction. From his experience of the plant recounted here, he appeals for more creative synthesis of this sort.

Bruce and his wife Sian came to the parish in the Notting Hill area straight from college at Oak Hill. Having seen this plant through they moved to the vicarage for Bruce to become vicar of Christ Church Roxeth where there was already one plant. Since his arrival the bishop gave him supervision of a group of 35 under a lady deacon to plant into the most unchurched estate in the diocese in a neighbouring parish. This has already grown to 80; Bruce now has plans to start their fourth plant under lay leadership within the parish. The church planting phenomenon seems to be a contagious sort of multiplication!

When I was first ordained in 1983, I was called to two parishes which had recently been linked together under one vicar. St Johns was of Anglo-Catholic tradition and drew a congregation of about 60 to 80 on a Sunday morning. The other parish, St Peters, was very much 'middle of the road' Anglican, drawing only 30 to 40 a Sunday. The two churches stand only 250 yards from one another, and there was a very real possibility that St Peters could be closed and made redundant.

I was trained at Oak Hill, and although I was of evangelical/charismatic churchmanship, I had looked at the curacy in Notting Hill because I felt I needed wider experience of the Church of England. I believe the Lord made it clear to me in several ways that he wanted me to go to St Johns and St Peters, and on the day I first walked into St Peters, I believe he said 'I want to do a new work in this place.'

That is my first point: in any work of church planting I believe it is essential that the leader of the plant, and if possible the sending church too, discerns a call from the Lord to embark on such a task, and hears his confirmation of when he wants this to commence. While I strongly believe that church planting is an essential if the church is going to have significant impact in making disciples in our nation, there is the commensurate danger that we can follow what may be fashionable in these times, without waiting sufficiently on the Lord to find out what, where, and when he wants things done. If we get it even partially wrong, we will dissipate energy, and hinder the growth of the church.

I arrived in Notting Hill in July 1983, and by the end of the year the apparently inevitable had happened – the St Peters congregation was amalgamated with St Johns. Believing that the Lord wanted to rebuild the St Peters congregation, I resisted this decision at first, until the Lord said to me 'New skins for new wine.' I came to understand that he wanted the new St Peters to be started on a completely new basis with a new core of people after the 'older wines' had been blended in St Johns. St Peters would have to become a new, flexible wineskin, able to cope with the immature, new wine the Lord wanted to bring in.

Over the next six months the PCC (consisting of members of the joint St Johns congregation) set up a feasibility study group to consider the future of St Peters, and it came up with a familiar proposal – to convert the upstairs galleries into space for commercial lettings, and use the ground floor as a community centre. Our architect drew up outline plans and costed the scheme at £450,000. Needless to say there was no prospect (or heartfelt commitment) to raise this kind of money.

During this period I had formed a small group of people which started meeting in St Peters on weekday evenings to worship, study the Bible and pray over the future of St Peters. My vicar, who was of liberal persuasion, was rather hesitant about the idea of planting a new congregation in St Peters, but was willing to give us his support provided we didn't seek to draw in any evangelical Christians from elsewhere. His reason, I think, was that he was concerned not to let the existing tradition of the parent congregation in St Johns be threatened by the growth of something too strongly evangelical in St Peters. This policy continued after the new congregation was planted in St Peters, and proved to be a great blessing to us, because it forced us to develop a mission which looked first to the needs of the local community, rather than attempt to meet the ecclesiastical tastes of the start-up team.

By late 1985 we came to believe that the Lord wanted the new plant to go ahead, and that we should simultaneously seek to develop new uses of St Peters which would build new links with the community. We prayed that he would confirm this through our vicar's agreement, and by giving us unanimous support in the PCC (a miracle, some felt, because there were several 'old' St Peters members on the PCC, who not unnaturally might have resisted others taking over the very lovely church building they had left so painfully only two and a half years earlier). I wrote an advance paper for the PCC, and after a long and very positive discussion in January 1986, the proposal was carried with only one abstention, so we decided to wait. After visits to reluctant people to explain the project in more depth and hear their concerns, I wrote another paper, and at its March meeting, the PCC gave us the unanimous decision we had prayed for. With hindsight we came to see the value of the waiting. It meant that the PCC had come to 'own' the new project. We also came to see the necessity of the two-and-a-half-year waiting period. This not only gave us time to clarify the vision and begin to form a team from scratch using local people, but it also gave time for 'old' St Peters to die, and allow the 'new' St Peters to be born.

We insisted that our little team of fifteen people was commissioned by the parent congregation, and sent out in prayer for our task, even though we were very aware that for most, the project was seen as an ambitious means of solving the problem of what to do with our other large and expensive building (St Peters was built to seat 1,400 people), rather than an evangelistic church plant.

We decided to hold 'practice' sessions for two Sundays before going public with leaflets through every door in the parish for a launch on Pentecost Sunday. Within a few Sundays we grew to 30 (still feeling very small in a building designed for 1,400, and I suspect even a member's dog got included in the congregation count for the service register!).

We obtained faculty permission to lift all the fixed wooden pews on the ground floor and convert them into moveable free-standing pews, in anticipation of buying chairs later when the money for this could be found. This allowed us to use St Peters for a wide variety of new activities: children's activities, plays, concerts, debates and even Scottish dancing one evening! This aroused considerable interest in the community, and much future growth came through contacts developed through these activities.

By the Lord's grace we saw steady growth: starting with fifteen at Pentecost 1986, we grew to a congregation of over 150 people who were regular members of St Peters. What gave me most joy was the fact that a very high proportion of this was conversion rather than transfer growth. We were also glad to see that virtually all our new growth came from people living locally. As mentioned earlier, if you are to build a community church, start with a nucleus of people from the immediate community.

This time in Notting Hill taught me several important lessons. I now know that the Lord loves to tell his people what he wants to do with them, usually, on the more important issues, well in advance. Waiting on him to clarify his will, and how he wants it carried out, is vital. I wasted so much time, burned much unnecessary energy, and caused unnecessary disagreements when I did not wait and listen for long enough.

These were not the only lessons I learned. My faith in the truth and power of God's word, and its central role in the building of his church, has been greatly deepened. I also saw in practice the immense value of what I had been learning through that period from John Wimber and others, who have been helping the church come into a practical understanding of what it means to participate in what remains the Lord's own New Covenant ministry, drawing on the gifts and power of his Spirit. We saw many drawn to the Lord and opened to the truth of the gospel through healings and other signs of the Kingdom.

I also came to discover that the Lord really can work in and through the structures of the Church of England! We received much practical help and encouragement from many quarters. I also found that the rather unusual mix of churchmanships (in what by 1990 had become the single parish of St John and St Peter) not only enriched our understanding and appreciation of differing liturgical traditions and churchmanships (and the differing psychological make-ups of their adherents), but also helped me to distinguish between what for me were truly matters of gospel conviction, and those things which represent different approaches to 'packaging' these convictions. I also believe that the fact that I was willing, as an evangelical, to wear a chasuble and even make smoke in services in St Johns was a vital factor in opening up the opportunity we were given in St Peters. We evangelicals can be too fussy about such things, and set up walls and barriers where they do not need to be built.

CHAPTER TEN

Forming Pastoral Bases in Brixton

Mike Breen

In many ways the story of Mike Breen and All Saints, Brixton Hill could be seen as another example of multiple congregation planting. It has similarities to what has developed at St Thomas, Crookes, as told in Chapter 3 – although here the congregations are on a much smaller scale, each being between 100 and 150 people. However, the really significant contribution is not what they have planted but how they have done it. There are some principles that Mike Breen shares here which can revolutionise the church and its evangelism. In many ways the plantings at All Saints have radically re-interpreted church growth models as applied in most other UK parishes. I see their strategy of 'bridge groups' and 'pastoral bases' truly achieving the aim of 'turning the church inside out'.

Step by step a pattern of church life and structures has evolved totally geared to getting Christians intimately interrelating with their non-Christian neighbours. Bridge groups and pastoral bases remind me of a cake recipe: 'Place all ingredients into a bowl – mix thoroughly and stir well until they reach an even consistency'!

I have described Mike's models as really radical. For some they may be too great a departure from their traditional patterns. It must be remembered that Mike and Sally have had their ministries formed in some of the most unreached parts of the British community – inner city and multi-racial youth. Their burning conviction that the gospel is as relevant and powerful for any group has led them to be prepared to re-examine and reinterpret any part of church life to serve only the two goals of mission effectiveness and faithfulness to scriptural principles. What they have developed from this has shown me that I am often so conditioned and blinkered by my tradition that I can only see scripture through the eyes of my familiar models of church.

In one sense, the planting of multiple congregations, all using the same building for their services, seems to go in the opposite direction to most church planting initiatives which step out of the church building and into community facilities in neighbourhoods. On the one hand Brixton is so dense a population that this is less of an issue. However, the much more significant fact is that All Saints has so radically broken the link between church and building that it becomes almost incidental where they happen to meet for any given part of their shared life of worship, fellowship and witness. They have refocused the whole thrust on the body of believers as the evangelising unit, with different congregational enter-prises directed to different sociological groups and neigh-bourhoods – each of which just 'happens' to continue to meet on Sundays/Thursdays in the same building – or at least does so for the immediate future!

Sally and I moved to All Saints, Brixton Hill, some four-and-a-half years ago. During that relatively short time we have seen the life of the church multiply in many different ways. The Lord has led us to some new patterns and principles which are still evolving and being proved in preparation for further multiplication. The key questions that God keeps challenging us with is: 'What kind of church are we planting?'; indeed, 'What is a church?'

When thinking about church planting, it may be

that we rarely stop to ask this sort of question. But if church planting is to be effective, this is perhaps the most fundamental question to be addressed. Often our thinking is based on our past experience, which arises from a church environment where 'church' is identified with a place and a Sunday event. Even in more 'enlightened' circles where church is not identified with a place, it is still identified with inflexible ideas and immovable expectations.

In short, our understandings of church are often static and religious. But these are not removed by making things more modern and up-to-date. Often all we do is replace an old religious experience with a new one. It would seem that some fresh thinking is needed if we are to ensure that what we plant and multiply is truly dynamic, alive and non-religious.

At All Saints, Brixton Hill, we have begun a process of challenging our own assumptions about what is fixed and what is changeable; what arises out of religion and what arises out of a relationship with God. As part of this we have begun to redefine our terms and renew our expectations of church growth and church planting.

I want to attempt to explain how we understand God leading us in this. But to appreciate what has happened at Brixton Hill and to relate its significance to more traditional patterns, I think it will help to tell the story of how some of the concepts developed in our previous ministry.

Changing the Style of Urban Youth Ministry

I completed a three year degree in theological and pastoral studies at Oak Hill in 1979. Then Sally and I moved to Hackney in the East End of London where

I was Youth Worker for two years. We lived in a flat on the Kingsmead Estate; over that period ours was the only unit not to be burgled. We followed the usual pattern of open youth work although most of our energies went into relating to the local youth on their ground. We then went to St John's, Durham for two years and I was ordained at the age of 25 in 1983. My first post was in Cambridge where I was attached to St Martins. This is in the 'down-town' end of Cambridge. After one year as curate I was appointed team leader of Romsey Mill. Four denominational churches had combined to sponsor a youth work programme and a redundant church building had been converted into a suitable facility for the project. I was responsible to a management committee who allowed me to form a team of workers. Together we built up the work until I experienced a major crisis in August 1985. I suffered third-degree burns in a gardening accident and was flat on my back for many weeks.

During those days of forced rest I had a dramatic new experience of God which proved to be a preparation and empowering for new things to come. Alongside this experience, as I reflected on our youth work to date, I was deeply dissatisfied. It seemed to me that although my heart lay in relationship-building with youngsters, the traditional structure of the open youth club did not seem to facilitate what I longed to see develop. In such youth clubs the 'leaders' were those with the biggest bunch of keys and the longest frowns – always to be seen rushing to protect or lock something up. They had to be quite brave and very highly trained to keep control and provide activities. In reality the effective leaders were usually the tough sixteen-year-old lads. As regards evangelism, we would get in the speakers who would withstand the jeers and cat-calls, and a few youngsters might get converted.

Alongside these experiences I was weighing new understandings from a number of sources. Firstly there was the Church Growth movement and their observations about the 'homogeneous unit principle' which said that groups of similar sorts of people are best for evangelism and grow fastest. Then there was the success of the Base Communities of Latin America where small self-determining groups grow together and have powerful effects on their neighbourhoods. Thirdly I reflected on Jesus' strategy for relationship-based evangelism as he instructed his disciples in the New Testament. In Matthew 10, Mark 6 and Luke 9, Jesus gives almost identical instructions to the twelve which correspond to those he gives to the seventy-two in Luke 10. I was surprised by how much there is about strategy here. Firstly Jesus affirms the strength of working in pairs. Then they are to go without resources, on their own – so depending on God for what he would provide and also, significantly, dependent on the people to whom they would go for food and shelter. They were to be vulnerable. This was the exact opposite of the 'provider and client' relationship on which I realised that all my youth work had been based.

Furthermore, the disciples were to look for and identify a 'worthy person' or 'man of peace' – someone open to them who received them and their message. These people would be the key access points into the community. They were to work with them in depth. In my book *Growing the Smaller Church*[1] I develop these principles further and show how the Acts accounts of Paul's church planting show that he worked according to the same strategy.

Out of the interaction between our past experiences and these new ideas, a new form of youth work and evangelism was born. We shut the open youth club and my assistant and I went to look for youngsters outside school or on the street who were responsive to us. We then asked who their friends (or peer group) were and asked what they would like to do together with them. First the 'provider/client' conditioning had to be broken as they asked 'What have you got?' and we replied 'Nothing – only what you and your friends can get together or organise.' So Alpha Groups were born – a kind of homogeneous unit with self-governing principles that encouraged initiative, responsibility and bonding in relationship.

These groups took off and were such a success that we had to work with waiting lists! Evangelism happened quite naturally as the two youth workers in each group just made friends and acted as facilitators. The life of Jesus in them rubbed off and provided natural questions. There were sometimes whole-group conversions. Another revolutionary aspect is the much lower requirements for youth workers – more of them are needed, but relatively untrained and with no special bravery!

Such was the fruit of this new approach that I expected that either we would have to become a Youth Church or one of the sponsoring churches on the management committee would have to change radically to accommodate all the new Christian youngsters in one of their congregations. Neither option was available, so we trained up replacements to take over our leadership roles and responded to God's next step for us.

The Move to Brixton and Proving 'Bridge Groups'

In the success of these Alpha Groups God began to show us that we were evolving a new model of evangelism which I came to call Bridge Groups: 'bridges', because they link together Christians and the unchurched community in a way that makes faith-sharing easy. The church goes to the community, rather than expecting non-Christians to come to us and do our thing. It's the Jesus strategy, in which we are the ones who become vulnerable and make relationships on their ground.

We felt this discovery to be so important that we wanted to test it out in a church growth/church planting situation. We looked for a large parish with a small congregation to make it easier to plant our new models of mission. As a result God led us to All Saints, Brixton Hill, where I became the vicar in 1987. Martin Lee, my assistant youth worker, moved with me from Cambridge. The parish population was some 10,000 and the existing congregation was about 40, thanks to foundation-laying by my predecessor. First we were keen to see if our youth work model would work in multi-racial Brixton. Here we call the units 'A Teams' and they are just as fruitful. In a short time we again had waiting lists and had to train more workers. The peer groups quite naturally were multi-racial, as that's the way the networks of friendship existed among the youngsters.

Encouraged by this repeated pattern of success we have seen the same bridge group principle work with senior citizens – where they may be called 'Retired and Refired' groups. We also have examples currently operating among young adults and African refugees. Then with single parent families we call them PACT Groups (Parent and Children Together). Within three years we had built up three congregations from this bridge-group evangelisation, each of which saw the small building at All Saints effectively full at 10 a.m., 11.30 a.m. and 7.00 p.m. The 10.00 a.m. is characteristically the older folk or professional people who have moved into 'gentryfied' housing on one side of the parish. The 11.30 a.m. is more predominantly young families (mainly single mums) and children, and the 7.00 p.m. a young/teenage service largely run by their own members. Our conclusion from all this is that New Testament evangelism was relationship-based. The New Testament church understood this and practised a model of evangelism given to them by Jesus, which flowed through relationships into the church.

If you extend the approach we had discovered to all areas of church life so that groups are formed among different age groups, friendship circles and family groups, you do not need to rely on an evangelistic strategy that depends on a fringe membership. Such an approach could even be used in a largely hostile environment, where only one or two contacts could be made.

If you are faithful to the commission of Jesus to reach the world, (including the apparently hostile places like inner cities) with his gospel, we need methods of evangelism that work well. In my opinion many of our most tried and trusted methods rely on a 'provider/client' relationship and usually some method of 'in-drag'. These facts alone severely limit our effectiveness. The strategy and methods of Jesus are based on different principles and produce better and longer lasting results.

Relationships are the channels of God's life. Making and maintaining relationships is a key skill that should be learned by all. In this way the strategy for the extension of the kingdom given by Jesus can be implemented by the whole church so that we begin to work like yeast in the dough.

Some of the 'Basics' of Bridge Groups

What is a bridge group?	A peer group or interest group, usually between 6–12 people.
How is it identified?	Through a 'man of peace'
How does it operate?	Self-programming, the group decides what they do.
Who leads it?	The natural leaders of the group
What do Christians do?	Serve the leaders and the group through inspiration and encouragement.

Changing the Life Direction in our Church Plants

One little experience in the establishment of the youth ministry at All Saints was something of a demonstration of the way we had not only developed a new way of outreach but were also radically changing what 'church' was. We had started a discipling meeting for the Christian young people converted out of the 'A Teams'. I happened to hear some of them saying they preferred this meeting and would stop going to their A Teams. I immediately closed the Christian discipleship meeting, to emphasise that it was only there to support and strengthen them in their A Team relationships with non-Christian friends – never as an opt-out into a 'Christian ghetto'!

This showed us that we had changed the direction of flow in the church structures we were planting. Many UK churches have introduced small group/cell life over the past 20 years, but usually their aim is to enrich congregational life by providing a small context for deeper sharing, Bible study, prayer together and ministry to one another – i.e. all inward activities and intended for life to flow up to an enriched congregation. The way we had been led was the reverse. The small group/cell life was primarily outreach-directed and the larger-unit life (more congregational in size) was there to enrich members and provide a flow of energy out to the cells which were in intimate inter-relationship with the world. Not only is the direction of flow changed – but so is the priority. Traditionally the congregation meeting on Sunday has been the most important grouping – the cell groups have strengthened this and helped it grow. However, we reflected on our experience, and on the success of the persecuted church in places like China where 'public' congregational services are impossible and the church seemed to flourish more not less! So we wondered whether the Sunday congregation service may not be the prime unit. This questioning and exploration has led on to the next development at All Saints that has emerged in the last 18 months.

But What is a Congregation?

I said above that from an extension of bridge evangelisation we developed/planted three congregations. But were these three Sunday services biblical congregations? In the introduction I explained that we have wrestled with the fundamental question of 'What is a church?' Now the Church Growth School have helped rediscover church life on three levels – celebration, congregation and cell. But have we too readily assumed that we know what each should be? I would venture to suggest that our ideas of congregation have been formed by 1,500 years of church history and tradition that has distorted the original biblical communities of which 'church' should be composed. Might what we call congregational life actually be more akin to celebration – after all, for centuries we have called the main service a 'celebration' of Eucharist/Mass. Let's look at the biblical roots.

The *celebration* level of community life was expressed in the major festivals and the temple worship. It was definitely a special occasion or outing – if not a pilgrimage sometimes! With this 'bigger-the-better' type of gathering anonymity is quite acceptable and it is essential to have a 'priestly' type of official or two, who lead and co-ordinate the procedure.

However the *congregation* level of life of the community of the people of God is more typified by the 'elders meeting in the gate' or the synagogue in Jesus' day and the New Testament mission period of Acts. This is altogether a more familiar group where everyone would know each other ('Isn't this Joseph's son?'). It was also an interactive gathering – that's why Jesus and Paul could read and preach/interpret as visitors – it was normal for anyone to freely contribute. It was often quite small with the requirement of just ten circumcised adult male Jews. The dynamics of its life should enable the working out of the word of God in the practical day-to-day life of the neighbourhood community.

Finally, the *cell* level of life was wonderfully expressed in the ideal of the Jewish extended family. Worship, word and prayer was natural in this context too – with the weekly Sabbath rituals including the sharing of bread and cup and of course the passover meal. (Interestingly – with reference to bridge groups – there was the requirement for a gentile outsider to be present for some gatherings of this cell unit).

With this in mind, we came to see that perhaps our

ideals of Sunday 'congregational' services were more truly in the celebration category. Through history we have focused all the proceedings on one or two 'up-front' leaders and created an expectation of anonymity. With our new model for cell groups and their relationship to the larger body, we were free to reinterpret congregational models that we could plant. From this the 'Pastoral Base' concept emerged as God led us.

Pastoral Bases – Establishing the Source of Life

In contrast to the bridge groups aimed at sociological strata, our Pastoral Bases were also focused on neighbourhoods in the parish. These are now the first places where 'church' takes place. We have sought to establish the life of All Saints in groups that meet on a weekly (week-night) basis. They are grown from the Christians in the programmes of small cell groups.

The pastoral base seeks to live out the descriptions of 'church', both in terms of worship and 'body life' found in the letters of the New Testament. Our aim is that they should be low-maintenance, low-tech, high-power gatherings of Christians who worship according to 1 Corinthians 14:26–33 and operate according to Ephesians 4:2–16.

Each member is encouraged to participate on equal terms, bringing a song, hymn, scripture, prophecy, instruction, etc. There is an expectation that as God's word is made clear to the group and to the individuals within it, he will provide the faith to follow him into the mission that he has revealed and prepared in advance (Romans 10:7, Ephesians 2:10).

The pastoral base is the natural place for the 'breaking of bread' to occur within the context of this informal worship structure. As an Anglican church, communion still takes place on the first Sunday of the month, but the regular sharing in 'agape meals' among members of the church takes place at the Pastoral Base. This informal and (hopefully) biblical programme means that the group can live a three-dimensional life. *Upward* in worship and prayer; *inward* in unity and fellowship; *outward* in compassion and evangelism. All three dimensions can and often do occur within the context of a single meeting. As the pastoral base comes together for prayer and worship this overflows into ministry to one another as needs are identified. Then members, usually in pairs, can go out from the group to do the thing that God has called them to do. Already these things are so diverse as to include painting a flat in a hard-to-let council estate, visiting shut-in and elderly people, prayer-walking around particular areas of their neighbourhood of the parish, door-to-door evangelism, running a basic Christian course and going swimming with a group of young people!

On completion of the activity the pairs return to their base to share their experience and to give and receive encouragement, have a hot drink and pray.

One base is so large that it meets in the church building as there are no houses big enough or robust enough to take 35–40 young people. When groups of this size have met in homes, distinct 'sittings' of prayer and worship have been needed, each initiating different phases of ministry and outreach.

High levels of activity and outreach do not occur every week, but rely on the work of God's Spirit working in the group to initiate and empower. Outside the group time each week, the members will be involved in specific relationship-building activities which are either formally organised or maintained informally through contacts with friends, neighbours and families.

Our understanding now is that our pastoral bases are *congregations* of All Saints church. We believe that the way they operate is closer to the New Testament pattern of congregational life (as explored above) than our Sunday Services.

Some of the 'Basics' of Pastoral Bases:

Leadership	2 or 3 trained, recognised leaders.
Membership	All those desiring to worship God, hear his voice and be discipled by Jesus.
How they Operate	Informally, corporately, biblically.
Activities	Worship, prayer, operating gifts of the Spirit, ministry and encouragement, outreach.
When and where	Dependent on time-availability of group, size of group, needs of group.
How big	From 6 to about 40.

Sunday Services

Once a pastoral base has been established and the means of initiating and maintaining relationships has been understood, a Sunday 'gathering' can be established. This is an opportunity to proclaim the gospel, through worship and word, on a weekly basis. It should involve those who are contacted through our work of relationship building in the community. These gatherings, usually meeting on Sunday, are for God – in that there is priority of worship – and for others – in that the proclamation of the gospel takes place each week. The Christians should not expect to have their needs met at this time, as they have their pastoral base where this can be done. As with other parts of the overall strategy, the service should be low-maintenance, low-tech, easily sustainable and self-propagating.

As such, the Sunday services are more akin to spreading our nets so as to catch fish than anything else. They are therefore geared to be user-friendly to outsiders. At All Saints we currently have four such gatherings. Each seeks to reach a specific set of people who have been identified by God to the church as our mission tasks at the moment.

a) Thursday night – 6–7 p.m. (children 3–12 years)
b) Sunday – 10.00 a.m. (senior citizens/young professionals)
c) Sunday – 11.30 a.m. (single parents)
d) Sunday – 7.00 p.m. (teenagers)

Each of these gatherings has its own style and communication but is supported by the same set of values. Each is served by two pastoral bases and a network of groups and informal relationships. Our expectation is that God will identify new groups and new locations to reach as we continue to seek his kingdom together in planting and multiplication.

Clearly these 'services' are temporary and not permanent, provisional and not static; and so change is expected, rather than resisted.

Conclusion

If we are to see rapid multiplication of churches we need a method of planting that works in all environments and with every people-group. I believe a strategy like the one outlined here may provide just such a method.

Also, for our methods to be easily transferable to other contexts, especially hostile environments which may increase, we must adopt low-maintenance, low-tech, high-power strategies. The heart of our planting model at All Saints is made up of:

1. *Relational evangelism* based on bridge groups that are the cell life of the church;

2. *Pastoral Bases* that seek to express New Testament congregational life amongst specific social groups or neighbourhoods; and

3. *Sunday services* which are celebrations but also have an emphasis on proclamation for the seeker.

Finally, God has also shown us that the sort of church we are planting should seek to be in real unity with others in our area of South London. He is leading us to work with the Baptists and Methodists to become together the church on Brixton Hill. To do this we need to share our resources and plant out ministry models where effective. Hence, we have given a secretary to the Baptists and trained youth workers for these other churches. We are also about to plant a Sunday evening 18–30s service in the Baptists' building and also to base the PACT groups with them.

CHAPTER ELEVEN

Planting in a New Housing Area

Anne Dyer

Perhaps the most obvious opportunity for Anglicans to church plant is where a whole new area of housing goes up. Here there are no cries of 'Why do we need another church? Haven't we got more than enough already!' The situation in Chatham may have been an obvious one for planting a new church, but the way that things developed involved experiences that were anything but obvious consequences of such a project.

This story complements the others since, like all authentic mission initiatives, it is quite unique; God's creative strategies are woven between the characteristics of the communities he sends us to reach and the individual personalities and gifts of those he calls.

Although much of this new housing area near Chatham is owner-occupied, this is not a middle class suburb and people's needs are just as near the surface as in many a UPA. Church planting onto new housing areas opens up the possibilities of ecumenical cooperation, and in this case both mother and daughter in the reproduction were Local Ecumenical Projects (LEPs). Like other church plants this project produces surprises. Although an Anglican-Methodist LEP meeting for much of its life in a hired pub room, the Dyers felt it important to establish familiar, identifiable symbols of worship for the very informal setting. Hence there were candles and they always wore cassock-albes. Anne Dyer, who tells this tale, is half of the husband-and-wife team that was ready to hear the call and pay the price of obedience to begin to lead this new emerging community in need of an ongoing redeeming presence. Significant therefore in their evangelism strategy has been the priority of winning whole families; making relationships with the whole unit which has already suffered enough dislocation and isolation.

Anne and Roger Dyer are both ordained. They started their ministry as curates in neighbouring parishes in Beckenham. Because of the problems of funding for women's ministry Anne received no stipend for her ministry there. To undertake this project they again accepted that they would only be able to receive one full stipend for both their full-time ministries in the plant.

The Church of Christ the King was planted by Christ Church, Luton (a Local Ecumenical Project) within its own parish three and a half years ago. It has met for worship in a community room above a pub, then in a school, and more recently in a new church building. During this period it has grown from a dozen worshippers to a congregation of over 200. Most of the growth has been through the conversion of family units, although many mature Christians of several denominations have joined the church. This year it has moved to being one of two churches in equal partnership in one parish. We have an overall team leadership of five people, made up of two of us on the estate, a Methodist minister and two other Anglican clergy at Christ Church.

The Area and People

The Princes Park estate, with a population of 10,000 and plans for a further 5,000, lies within the parish of Christ Church, Luton, in Chatham one of the Medway Towns. When this greenfield site was designated a new housing area in the late seventies, the Diocese of Rochester purchased a small plot of land at what turned out to be the centre of the new estate. The intention, through the next fourteen years or so, was to build a church on that estate at the right time.

The first buildings erected on the estate were low-quality council units, to provide accommodation for overspill families from the Greater London Council. The condition of these units has deteriorated greatly in the last decade. The families living in them are among the most needy in the Medway Towns. There is a higher than average incidence of unemployment, single parent families and all types of abuse within this part of the estate.

From the mid-eighties onwards, a second phase of private housing developed. The majority of these houses are small units: one or two bedroom starter homes. These sold quickly, although many of those who bought them have found meeting mortgage payments difficult, and could not afford to move to more suitable accommodation when children were born.

Most of the families on the estate have young children. They have moved into a new area without adequate facilities of any kind, whether nurseries, transport, schools or shops, and have become cut off geographically and emotionally from support from their extended family. Loneliness and depression are rife.

Phase I: Church Planting

The church plant from Christ Church into this estate began three and a half years ago. Christ Church is itself an Anglican-Methodist LEP, and before planting a congregation, invited all denominations in the area to participate in the project. Although the other churches were verbally supportive, only the Anglican and Methodist churches were able to commit resources to it.

The new church would be the only one on the estate, so a commitment to a wide ecumenical base was vital. It has been an important principle of the new church that all Christians should be welcomed and affirmed, and work together to build the kingdom of God. The church itself has had three phases in its short life, marked by changes in location for worship.

Three families living on the estate were worshipping at Christ Church. They were asked if they would begin to worship locally, supported by teams from the parish church. They began to worship in a community room above a pub. It was not an attractive place to meet. On a Saturday night, people would have parties, and on a Sunday morning there would often be a residue of unsavoury debris from the previous evening. The strategy of the first year was simply to establish a Christian presence, and by the end of it there were about 20 adults. The most significant thing was that local Christians were working together to set up a room for worship, something that looked like a church.

Both myself and my husband are ordained, and had been working in separate parishes elsewhere. At the end of this first year, we were licensed as ministers-in-charge of this congregation. We moved into a house purchased by the diocese. The house is not parsonage standard, but is nevertheless twice the size of most houses on the estate. We are working on just one stipend, but still have more disposable income than most people on the estate. For us, there was a cost involved in moving in to lead the planting team.

We were shocked at first at the state of the church. It was wonderful that it existed; but the facilities were very poor. For example, many people on the estate were in their early to mid-thirties and had young children. Worshipping with everyone together, including a dozen toddlers, in one small room was very difficult. The worship was, in our opinion, sub-standard. Music was very rudimentary.

We therefore quickly made two decisions. One was to move to a local school, even though we could not afford it. We believed that if we moved to a place with better facilities, more people would come and our income would increase. Secondly, we looked for someone to take responsibility for the music. We found someone from the parent church, who now lives on the estate with us.

Phase II: In the Local School

The school proved very suitable. Most of the children that came were there during the week. The mothers and fathers knew the school well, and it was not at all threatening. People found it very accessible, and we grew significantly.

During this second stage, we re-assessed our priorities. The first priority was to worship God. Although the social needs in the area were so pressing, we felt worship should come first. We could easily have been sucked into just meeting people's human needs. We might have missed out worshipping God, which was our vocation and what we had been sent there to do.

We felt that worship should be contemporary in

style and accessible in content, especially for people who cannot read or whose only reading is popular newspapers. Continuity with the culture of everyday life is very important. Being an LEP has been a great help in this, as we are not restricted to Anglican patterns of worship, but can use a wide range of Nonconformist service patterns.

If worship is to be accessible, then all worship should be. We were forced to question what we were doing at communion services. We obtained our bishop's permission to have an open table: otherwise, 95% of people would be excluded. We invite anyone who wants to follow Jesus Christ in their life during the coming week to receive the bread and wine with us. We have been very grateful for the great freedom we have in this; and people appreciate knowing that they are equally welcome at every service, and can participate fully in the body of Christ.

The next priority was fellowship. The people in our area are poor, and there is no sense of community. Young families have moved in either under pressure from the council, or attracted by the cheap housing. They have lost their extended family and their friends. We felt we needed to make a social life within our community. We planned monthly social events for the whole family, either free or at a very low cost. People have been able to relax with us, and do not feel that we are pursuing them. There have been cricket, football, quiz nights, and so on; and the result has been that whole families have come on Sundays.

We have therefore seen whole families coming to Christ, and this has fitted with our general strategy of evangelism. The aim has not been to win individuals, which would risk drawing them out from their families, and cause further dislocation of whatever com-

munity did exist in people's homes. Rather, the aim
has been to win whole family units.

Neither my husband nor myself are evangelists; and
we were helped by three visits from the evangelist J.
John. Each time he came for a week. People were not
converted there and then, but they were helped to
articulate whatever they were experiencing in the fellowship and in the worship. This is the kind of evangelism which has been meaningful in our situation.

Phase III: Into a Church Building

During all this time, the diocese of Rochester was
planning a building for us. Originally, they
approached an architect who came up with what
seemed to them a wonderful plan: a very attractive
piece of building, which would seat 80 people. That
had been the extent of the vision. At that stage, we
were already too big for such a building. Furthermore,
it was going to cost one and a half million pounds.
Naturally, we questioned the rightness of this plan.

The Church of Christ the King was the last to qual-
ify for a new housing area grant from the Church
Commissioners. Their gift of £250,000 was matched by
Rochester Diocese. There was therefore half a million
pounds available; and eventually a design and building company was commissioned to construct a church
building including community rooms, on the site purchased fourteen years before, at a total cost of just less
than half a million pounds. The building will seat up
to 600 people. This was the kind of vision we had for
the church in our community. The building went up in
seven months, causing quite a stir in the community.

As the council, in their planning of the area, had
not allowed for any community facilities at all, this is
the only community building on the estate. Sometimes

on estates one has to question whether a new building is right, but for us it was the right thing to do.

In the month in which we moved in we did three things. First, we moved the congregation from the school to the church. That was in fact quite traumatic for them, because they were happy in the school. The school had a sloppy feel to it; and it was nice for people, if they were a bit untidy at home, to come into those surroundings. Coming to a spanking new church building, where the seats were in rows, has been difficult for a lot of our people.

Second, we opened the church to the community. We had an open week to which we invited every person on the estate; and hundreds came to have a look. Third, we used the contacts we made on the open week during a mission with J. John.

In that three-week period we added 60 people. It was quite frightening, suddenly having 60 new people, bearing in mind that the original church was only about 140, and many of them had only been coming for a year. We have very few mature Christians.

All this has made us very bold. We have always believed in preaching the gospel, but now we do not hold back at all. Preaching the gospel has become very easy, and people – especially young people – have been longing to hear. It has been a very exciting time.

We have been able to add to our priorities, and to begin offering service and support to those living on the estate. We now have resources to offer, both in people and in building facilities. We are trying to discover what God is asking of us now, in an area of very great need.

Conclusion

There have been several lessons for us as ministers, in the last two and a half years. The first has been that each phase of the church's life requires a new strategy. This requires flexibility and openness of thinking, and above all a determination to find and follow God's agenda. Second, we have learnt that changes – in our case, moves – are made *before* we have the resources to meet our needs. If a change is right, then growth follows which frees the necessary resources.

Third, planting and growth involves movement towards a vision given by God. This involves risk, change and uncertainty. Team leaders in this situation need to be people who can cope with this. Someone who finds change disturbing would find this a very difficult job, because once they found a comfortable stage, they would want to remain there. Moving on is actually the healthy thing to do. We have found this for ourselves as a couple ministering together, and for us as a people desiring the coming kingdom of God.

It has been a tense time for the team leadership. When we arrived, my husband and I were pastoring a church of 20, so we were the vulnerable ones in the team. We are now pastoring a church as big as the church which planted us. The way staff meetings work has had to change. Clergy working together do not manage changing relationships very well. They threaten each other very easily, and this has been a big issue for us. If a church grows very quickly, the relationships change as well, and one needs to be aware of that.

CHAPTER TWELVE

Twenty Years On: Chester-le-Street Today

As I explained in the Introduction to this book, Chester-le-Street was one of the 'fore-runners' of the present wave of 'new style' Anglican church plants. Back in 1971 in County Durham in the North East, they started the first of what was to multiply to six satellite congregations. This is a large town comprising a single parish of some 25,000 souls. The church planting mission strategy was intended to more adequately reach this large and differentiated area and was initiated by the then vicar, Patrick Blair. We start with the assessment of the experience by the third vicar in the process, the present incumbent Geoffrey Walker, who inherited the seven-area congregations. His story is then followed by reflections on the maturing process by the vicar of the mid years when most of the planting occurred – Ian Bunting. Their accounts provide different views of the same process, but both draw a range of helpful conclusions from the consolidation of such long-term church planting. They are agreed that the speed of multiplication may have led to insufficient time being given to communication with the diocese.

I like the way that Geoffrey Walker is allowing the different area congregations to further develop their distinct identities in response to their neighbourhoods, their resources and the presence of other denominational groups. It is particularly good to see the flexibility of approach to consider a midweek evening worship service in the area of highest unemployment.

*However, I hope that such creativity and continued commit-
ment to appropriate outreach will prove that we do not have
to be limited by national norms of percentage attendance for
a particular socio-economic group. I believe that when such
a norm is as low as 1.5%, then church planting mission
initiatives are showing that this can change. As Geoffrey
reflects on the reasons for the loss of growth in several of the
areas, I can't help wondering if one contributing factor may
not be that the parish boundary has limited natural expansion once seven congregations were established. In any event,
the ability to reflect on over 20 years of planting into distinct
neighbourhoods can give helpful pointers and invaluable
experience for those beginning similar models of mission
elsewhere.*

I: Reassessing the Vision

Geoffrey Walker, Chester-le-Street

When I came to Chester-le-Street in late 1987, I
inherited a parish which had undergone, in the previous 20 years, a revolution in church life. Through
the guidance and inspiration of my two predecessors,
Patrick Blair and Ian Bunting, the local church had
experienced an explosion in evangelistic outreach,
which had led to the establishment of seven area
Family Services. This explosion was accompanied by
a corresponding growth in the real participation of lay
people in almost every aspect of Christian life, both
within and beyond the confines of the church community.[1]

By the mid-eighties, what had been a traditional
and largely dormant Anglican parish had emerged as

a torch-bearer on the national church planting scene. Books, such as Eddie Gibbs' *Ten Growing Churches* (1984), described the principles of church growth which had directed the vision of the church in Chester-le-Street in the previous fifteen years. Chester-le-Street, with its staff team and league-topping diocesan quota, was a star of the Durham diocese.

However, there were a number of clouds forming on the horizon. Some of these motivated a parish audit undertaken by the late Canon John Poulton over a number of months in 1985. Others emerged as a consequence of that report. It's worth mentioning the more important of these as the background to more recent developments in the parish.

First, the 'bleeding church', the phenomenon experienced by all the area Family Services, where new growth is cancelled out by those who leave, or where newcomers are difficult to keep. There was a decline in numbers of those committed to regular worship by comparison with those who came at the 'high water mark' of church membership in the early eighties. Second was the question of the 'monochrome church', created by the perceived evangelical monopoly in a community where parish and town are synonymous and where many were concerned about the lack of main-service eucharistic worship. And third, the diocese was uneasy about the use of lay people in leading worship and in preaching. The whole subject of 'authority' between area family congregations worshipping in unlicensed buildings, and the extent of the jurisdiction of the diocese over them, was to lead to difficulties.

The overall impression I received when coming to the parish in 1987 was of a church which had begun to lose some of the original vision which had inspired its growth. It was eagerly seeking new ways of moving forward, but lacked any real sense of direction. That

was not surprising, because churches go through life-
cycles, and the ending of one phase of life is often the
means whereby a renewal takes place.

Early in my ministry the PCC undertook an 'Area
Family Service Review'. This took the form of a questionnaire, and was partly a parish audit, and partly
an opportunity to 'dream dreams'. It confirmed some
of the findings of the Poulton report, and highlighted
a number of factors. These have formed the basis for
more recent developments. Significantly, we discovered that different areas were saying different and
sometimes contradictory things:

1. The appropriateness of the 'strawberry plant' model was called into question

Three areas (Pelaw, West, and Pelton Fell) asked for
greater interdependence, and this trend has been
reinforced by opportunities for meeting and fellowship
which have been provided by the parish centre.

One area (Hermitage) is now actively seeking to
build a church on derelict land in a part of the town,
which could in time become either a daughter church,
a Conventional District, or a parish in its own right.
Significantly, the site proposed would take in the
whole of the West area, as well as several hundred
newly-built houses which will link Waldridge Village
and Chester Moor to the rest of Chester-le-Street. All
the signs are that the Hermitage and West area congregations will cooperate in this project, with the support and encouragement of the PCC. There is a possibility that the Chester Moor congregation might
become involved as well, and it is anticipated that
the non-Anglican churches in Chester-le-Street will be
invited to join in.

North Lodge area continues to meet in the comprehensive school, and is pursuing an independent line.
Central area, which meets in the parish church, has

no discernible area consciousness whatsoever. The majority who worship there do so because it is the parish church, even though many live outside the central area.

2. The original vision has been lost in most areas

There is still a desire to see God's kingdom grow, and his name blessed, although how this is to happen is open to question. An expressed wish for more teaching, or for clergy to stay longer, seems to be the way in which most congregations are attempting to articulate the view that things are not as they should be. Much of the perceived vision from the past appears to focus on the ministry of certain individual clergy, which was lost to sight when they left.

The response over the past eighteen months (since late 1989) has taken a number of forms. Broadly speaking, four major initiatives have helped to shape an emerging vision for the nineties. First, a renewed emphasis on Christian stewardship. Second, the implications for Christian life and witness of a new parish centre, due for completion by the end of the 1991. Third, a major parish mission, with a focus week in mid-June 1991. And lastly, a 'year of Jubilee' from mid-1991 to mid-1992, when no major new projects will be started and in which the emphasis will be on establishing the right basis for area family ministry for the future.

Of these, the first three have a strong area emphasis. The parish mission, for example, has shied away from any big, town centre events, and is taking place in areas using the worship centres as the venues. Each area family service is running its own mini-mission, within the context of a parish-wide event.

3. Declining numbers, and the needs of the congregations

In every area, the number of worshippers declined between 1984 and 1989. The decline is particularly marked amongst children and men. Congregations are getting older; and a significant percentage of many congregations is made up of those who were the original church planters. On the basis of national percentages of those in a given area who can be expected to be in an Anglican place of worship on a Sunday, some of the area catchments are simply too small. Pelton Fell and West areas in particular may have reached that point of entropy from which church growth is unlikely. Since 1989, there has been a marked increase in the size of congregations at Hermitage and North Lodge – Hermitage, for example, is up by 50%, mostly adults – with a corresponding decline at Pelton Fell and West areas. Pelaw is starting to grow again, while Central area remains fairly static.

The diet of worship, despite the apparent freedom to experiment, remains predictable and 'churchy'. Since 1989 there has been an increase in the numbers attending traditional worship at the parish church, sometimes by as much as 30%, largely made up of those who attend an area family service. The introduction of regular opportunities for Eucharistic worship in the areas has led to a marked increase in adults coming forward for confirmation, and a corresponding rise in communicants at the parish church.

Relations with the diocese have improved, with the introduction of Area Service Leaders, commissioned by the bishop, and the establishment of canonically-sanctioned arrangements for worship in unlicensed buildings.

The Case of Pelton Fell

Pelton Fell's response to the audit was interesting. They have recognised that there is no longer a role for traditional Christian ministry in an area of high deprivation and social need. The impact of Sunday morning worship within a community, most of whose members are still in bed, is questionable. Statistics show the minimal impact of the church over the years in anything but first aid, crisis ministry. Taking 1½% as the norm for attendance at worship within a population of a given size, the likelihood of significant future growth is limited. If the *raison d'être* for a planted service at Pelton Fell is simply that there was once a mission church there (it was demolished 20 years ago) then, taken together with the other points, the continuance of the Pelton Fell area ministry in its present form is questionable.

Pelton Fell Pilot Group have taken several steps as a result. First, they have initiated a project in cooperation with others in the community for a full-time youth and community worker. A village appraisal was undertaken in 1989, and this came to involve a cross-section of the local community including many with whom the church had not previously had contact. The need for a youth and community worker was established, and received support from the District Council and from the Church Urban Fund. All going well, Pelton Fell will have its full-time worker by the end of 1991.

Second, they plan to discontinue the Sunday service, and replace it with a mid-week afternoon service, building on the success of a mother and toddler group set up in 1989. In an area with high male unemployment, they argue that the change of time will enable more men to come, especially where there is some attempt at joint parenting, while recognising the social realities of Sunday morning in a traditional and depressed working-class area. Third, the existing Pelton Fell congregation is looking forward to the opportunity to worship with other Christians on a Sunday morning, at a well-attended and properly resourced service in another part of the town.

Conclusions

The establishment of the area family services over the past 20 years will continue to set the agenda for much of the Christian work in the parish of St Mary and St Cuthbert, Chester-le-Street. There is a clear desire to see these services as the building-blocks of outreach into the communities of the town. However, the number and arrangement of area services may have to change in response to new insights.

The church in Chester-le-Street, 20 years ago, was convinced that the pattern of the past should not be allowed to dictate the shape of the future. We find ourselves in the same position today. The past must not be allowed to become inhibiting. It was never the intention of those who set out to achieve the vision of the seventies and eighties, that their ideas should have any permanence beyond that of serving God's world in ways appropriate to their time. We want to honour that vision by evolving a pattern of Christian life and witness in Chester-le-Street which is appropriate to God's world now.

II: Reflections Twenty Years On

Ian D. Bunting

I have three reflections on the strategy of church planting in Chester-le-Street, which began 20 years ago.

First, the concept of growing churches which are *from, of*, and *with* Christians at the grassroots is soundly based. It rings true to the gospel. It is right for the Christians of a neighbourhood, or a community network, to provide a corporate Christian presence, to take responsibility within the community, and to offer a credible witness to Christ there.

Second, it is important to keep in close touch with the leaders of the diocese. They are busy people; but we did not take sufficient care to ensure that they were fully informed about what was happening. We should have taken more trouble to gain their interest and participation throughout the process. We would thereby have avoided some problems.

Third, Anglican leaders at diocesan level are in a good position to promote church planting, but often fail to do so. One reason is that they fear loss of control. In practice, they do not welcome the idea of subsidiarity: that is, the view that the best decisions and actions are initiated at the lowest level in the organisation. Leaders who believe in genuinely collaborative ministry will, like midfield football players, serve their strikers: the church planters.

Another reason is the fear of grassroots ecumenism.

While leaders usually welcome ecumenical efforts, they tend to regard with suspicion those Christians who engage in church planting with scant respect for denominational labels. Local church planting is always likely to be ecumenical in its appeal. When we say that the Anglican church is parish-based, we accept a responsibility for the whole community; and it is possible to establish local structures and patterns of worship which are not contrary to Anglicanism.

There is also a blinkered view of evangelism. Anglican leaders seem to have a commitment to maintain parochial church-based evangelism, which can limit the nature and range of the gospel we can proclaim. It is inappropriate to an urbanised nation such as ours. A loosening up, and an authorising of structures for mission, would enable us to evangelise a wider cross-section of the population than we are capable of reaching at present. Where there is an episcopal will, there is a way.

Finally, Anglican leaders suffer from the intransigence of the clerical sub-culture from which they have emerged. They not only find it hard to escape hierarchical views of leadership, but their sometimes defensive decision-making can perpetuate the competitive spirit which is endemic within Anglican clergy. This is a glaring paradox, because on appointment they usually try to shed any earlier prejudices they may have had in order to encourage all the clergy and every ministry in their diocese.

In short, we are both an episcopal and a parish-based church. The cure of the local church is a shared responsibility. As Anglican leaders collaborate with each other in their episcopal ministry, so they have a marvellous opportunity to help others shed the defensiveness which dogs many clergy and inhibits some new Anglican mission initiatives.

PART THREE

Church Planting – the Wider View

CHAPTER THIRTEEN

A Time to Plant – Recent Church Planting Statistics

George Lings

For any movement to succeed it needs not only its practitioners and enthusiasts but also the 'brains' behind it all! George Lings is definitely one of the brains that God has given to the network of Anglican church planters. For the past six years George has acted as 'official statistician' for all known Anglican church plants. He has kept records on a database developed on his computer. He acknowledges that his records are incomplete since he only has records where people have informed us – or when we have 'stumbled across' planting ventures. To try to make the data as comprehensive as possible George has put notices in The Church Times *and the* Church of England Newspaper. *We have also sent round circulars and asked to be informed if any in the church planting network learn of a new plant. Nonetheless we keep hearing of plants that started several years ago that are not in our figures. If you feel that your plant or one known to you could have been omitted from the following statistical survey, please write to George Lings, 8 St George's Road, Deal, Kent. He would be delighted to hear from you.*

George not only keeps the records but is an analyst of church planting in the Church of England. Together, we have developed grids for classifying the different models of plant and he regularly produces new questionnaires to incorporate new categories. However, his work does not stop there, because I believe that as he reviews the historic data of Anglican plants over the last 25 years, he brings to the information a prophetic gift for assessing their significance and discerning the future challenge to our church. This challenge needs to be heard and responded to at every level.

George first got a vision for church planting while a senior curate at St Mary's Reigate where there was significant church growth. His desire to see these resources channelled into church planting mission shaped his strategy when he felt God calling him and his wife Helen to move on from Reigate. He could see a potential team of more than half a dozen folk who were ready to consider moving with him to any location within a commuter distance of London so that they could keep their jobs. George wrote with this proposal to ten bishops in the dioceses in and around the capital. Most were negative or didn't seem to understand the proposal. Two looked at it seriously but were unable to suggest a suitable planting project. With this door closed he later moved in 1985 to his present post as vicar of St George's parish, Deal in Kent. Again there has been growth with the congregation rising from some 150 to 250. This has involved informal cell plants being negotiated with the incumbents of the other 3 parishes in the town.

The present high level of interest in church planting is a welcome change. But the danger is that stereotypes are formed and needless battle lines drawn. There is a need to examine the evidence: where are the plants? Why are they there? What size are they? Do they threaten parish boundaries?

Where are the Plants?

Some imagine that church plants are exotic: flowering only in a hot-house atmosphere of charismatic worship, watered by eclectic congregations drawn to famous city-centre churches. But in reality, Anglican church plants occur in all kinds of areas or districts: in town and country, in suburbs and inner city. Certainly, they occur in places where the Church of England has traditionally been strong: the suburbs, towns, private housing estates, city centre locations, villages expanded into dormitory areas, and estates mixing local authority and private housing. But plants have also grown up in areas in which Christian ministry has been tough going, each for its own variety of reasons: the Urban Priority Areas, inner urban districts, on local authority estates, in new towns and rural communities. Figure 1 shows that church plants occur in all types of district. True, the single largest entry is for the suburbs, but it would be unfair to the evidence to consider 22% of the plants as normative.

The balance of church plants between strong church-going places, and places regarded as 'tough', is 55% to 45%. If the mixed local authority and private estates are counted as tough as well, then the split would be 50% each. Bearing in mind that church planting is an uncoordinated grass roots movement, it is remarkable that it has occurred throughout urban Britain. An apparently spontaneous movement, it stands firmly in the Anglican tradition of mission responsibility for the nation – not feathering the nest of 'comfortable Britain' – to borrow Bishop David Sheppard's phrase.

Rural Lock-Out?
Rural England has hitherto been untouched by plants.[1] Why this exception? It is hard to plant in scattered, overchurched communities, for lack of obvious and acceptable leaders. Rural ecclesiology and village expectations tend to make the clergyman a tame chaplain to the community. These, along with pressure on clergy to be a kind of mobile Eucharistic vending

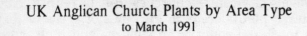

Figure 1

UK Anglican Church Plants by Area Type
to March 1991

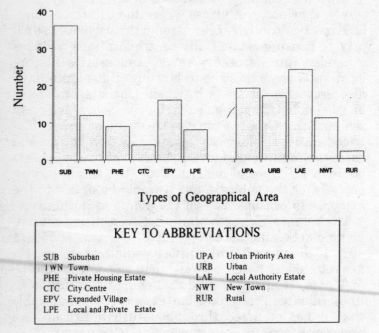

Types of Geographical Area

KEY TO ABBREVIATIONS

SUB	Suburban	UPA	Urban Priority Area
TWN	Town	URB	Urban
PHE	Private Housing Estate	LAE	Local Authority Estate
CTC	City Centre	NWT	New Town
EPV	Expanded Village	RUR	Rural
LPE	Local and Private Estate		

machine, militate against church planting. It is not that there is no need, simply that no way has been found through the cultural and ecclesiological jungle of the rural area.

Motives for Planting

What has prodded Anglican church planters into action? We have noted six separate strands of motive and seen a changing pattern across three chapters of

Anglican post-war church planting history (see figure 2):

Figure 2

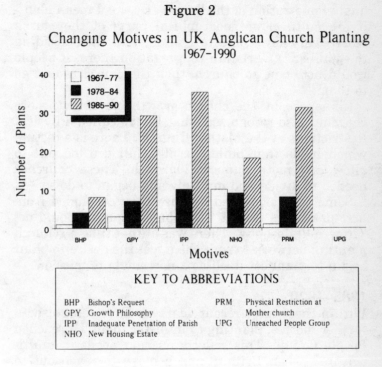

Changing Motives in UK Anglican Church Planting
1967–1990

1967–1977

In this period, the leading motive was new housing opportunities, which accounted for half the instances. My interpretation is that early planting was entertained most easily when virgin territory was in sight. Thus, the fiction of the country being covered for mission purposes by the parish system still remained intact and unchallenged. Today, that motive trails in fourth place – a mere 14% of the last six years' planting – despite the vigorous growth of further new housing until 1989.

1978–1984

During these seven years, other mission motives moved into the spotlight. Top of the list came 'Inadequate Penetration of the Parish'. By this I mean identifying cultural or geographical parts of the parish where very few come to church, and then deciding to establish a Christian congregation there. If people would not come to church, then the church would go to them.

Influenced by the church growth movement, more churches also recognised what I have called 'Physical Restrictions at the Mother Church'. There is a dictum which holds that buildings 80% full are too full to allow any more numerical growth. These churches needed to divide and multiply and began to do so.

Some others planted because they concluded from first principles that it was what a church should do: 'Growth Philosophy'. There was at that time no church planting network to spur them, yet the desire to plant began to manifest itself as a new angle to mission.

1985–1990

Within these most recent years we have recognised a further motive, planting to minister to an 'Unreached People Group'. This reflects mission needs in multicultural urban Britain, and a move to reach out to ethnic and youth cultural groups.

However, over the last six years, inadequate penetration of the parish, physical restriction at the mother church, and growth philosophy, continue to be the leading motives, and each must be taken seriously. It is clear that there is still some slack in the parish system to be taken up, and churches are wanting to take their parish mission calling thoughtfully.

But what of full churches, with congregations committed to growth, which exist within small parishes? Technically they have nowhere else to spread out to.

Is it right or wise that they should be muzzled in the name of church order? Can that be squared with serious commitment to a decade of evangelism?

Throughout, a lead from the top has played a small part in motivation. Where diocesan initiative enters, it is nearly always where pastoral reorganisation or greenfield site housing has been involved. Bishops and dioceses are rarely coming forward with radical mission strategies, but rather reacting to problems. If only more dioceses would dare to follow Salisbury's example, which recommended in print that congregations of 200 or more should actively consider church planting.[2] That move would provoke the parish boundary question yet more sharply, as shall be seen below.

Plants and Anglican Structures

To Rent or to Own

What sort of buildings are commonly used? The public rented unlicensed building is the most frequent, for simple reasons. It is immediately available, and cheap to rent and operate. It is neutral territory (a useful asset in unchurched areas). There are few complications when a move to something larger is needed.

Ecclesiastically-owned licensed buildings are the second choice. These are mainly inherited buildings, either already declared redundant, or tiny congregations under threat of closure.

As time goes on, a tendency develops to build a specific ecclesiastical building for the plant. The congregation can then control its affairs, and the move appeals to deep English instincts for the proper way: it becomes a 'real church', and perhaps even a parish in time.

Boundary Matters

Boundary disputes are reputedly the most common source of work for solicitors, and seem to generate similar heat in church affairs. But how have church plants related to parish boundaries in the 20 years?

1) Over seven out of every ten church plants occur within the existing parish

Figure 3

Buildings, Boundaries, Mission and Ecumenical Status
of UK Anglican Church Plants (March 1991)

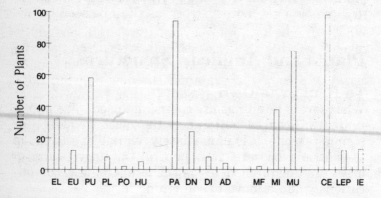

KEY TO ABBREVIATIONS

Buildings
EL.   Ecclesiastical Owned. Licensed
EU   Ecclesiastical Owned. Unlicensed
PU   Public Rented. Unlicensed
PL.   Public Rented. Licensed
PO   Public Owned
HU   House. Owned. Unlicensed

Boundaries
PA   Within the Parish
DN   Within the Deanery
DI   Within the Diocese

AD   Across Diocesan Boundaries

Mission
MF   Mission Area, Formally
MI   Mission Area, Informally
MU   Mission Area, Unrecognised

Ecumenism
CE   Church of England
LEP   Local Ecumenical Project
IE   Informal Ecumenical Project

2) At least nine out of every ten church plants fall within the existing deanery.

3) Less than one out of every ten church plants has arisen beyond the deanery or across a diocesan boundary.

Moreover, 96% of the known plants (perhaps 150 examples) went ahead with nothing less than full diocesan consultation and permission, despite the media association between church planting and boundary-breaking.

Church Planting Beyond the Parish Boundary

What do church plants beyond the parish boundary reveal? In a third of cases, the plant occurred to serve new housing that spanned two adjoining parish boundaries. In a couple of examples the new housing even crossed diocesan boundaries. In other instances pastoral reorganisation left a nearby surplus building, or joined two parishes: both circumstances which invited a plant. In a quarter of occurrences the diocese took some initiative. It all seems innocuous, and in any case the cross-boundary plant is a minority case.

But there are storm-clouds on the horizon. In the last five years, the number of full churches wanting to grow, but without spare territory, has increased. These are in the conurbations where people are mobile and choose their church by perceived relevance, not by parish boundary. Such choice is irreversible. And the figures show that cross-boundary planting is a growing trend:

1967–77	22%
1978–84	26%
1985–90	28%

This trend will continue, not least because church planting is the single fastest form of church growth. By definition, those parishes which embark upon church planting in their parish will run out of parish space fastest. The number of parishes which are on their second or third plant are proof of this. They are on a collision course with the rigid parish boundary, irrespective of their motive or ecclesiology.

Church planting, unintentionally, could be the single largest challenge to the parish system since John Wesley. My prayer is that we shall not repeat the mistakes of history and unchurch our pioneers. I hope that those with the power to work to make the system more flexible will do so.

The 'mission status' of church plants is indicated on figure 3, and this may indicate a way forward. Local Ecumenical Projects (LEPs) and suspended livings are familiar ground for Anglicans, and the concept of a Local Mission Area may be possible within the Pastoral Measure. Although most planters work with their assessment of the mission needs of a potential planted area unacknowledged, there is hope: mission areas were in some sense formally recognised in three recent plants. It is an encouragement to note that a third of plants are informally seen as tackling discernible districts needing evangelisation.

Ecumenism

Does ecumenism fit with Anglican church planting? In most cases it does not. Ecumenism appears to offer a flexible response in worship to the people of an unchurched area. But the lengthy, even tortuous, establishment period, ecumenical bureaucracy, and the levelling down of distinctives, can seem like hindrances easily outweighing any benefits.

Are LEPs included in planting data? It depends, for LEPs can fall into two distinct categories. One kind is a joint venture in a new town, or among new housing on a green field site. There, it makes splendid sense not to perpetuate denominationalism or to multiply tiny, struggling congregations. Where these are known, we gladly include them, and suspect there are more not known to us.

The other kind is a merger of threatened local firms. These uneasy alliances in the face of decline are not included as church plants.

Do We Need More Congregations?

A startling and alarming set of figures were collated for 1974 by Rev'd David Wasdell of the Church Urban Project.[3] He researched and plotted the size of average congregations in parishes of a given size. As one would expect, with larger parishes, congregation sizes do creep up. But any proportionate increase occurs only over a very limited range of small parishes and there are vital qualifying remarks.

He found that it made little difference to congregation attendance whether a parish was 6,000 or 15,000 (see figure 4). 200 appears an absolute barrier for a single congregation led by a sole clergyman, which is still the typical situation in the urban parish. Wasdell found that any further increase was directly attributable to additional staff, irrespective of parish size. This is an argument for more smaller churches to be planted from large ones that have over 200 members.

Yet more significant for church planting is the diminishing line showing the percentage of church attenders for each parish size. As the parish size increases it is obvious that the church becomes utterly ineffective in reaching its parish. For example, a parish of 2,000 may reach 10% of its people: a proportion that is visible and a group which has a continuing credible impact on its community. But by contrast 2% in 10,000

Figure 4

Diminishing Penetration of CE Parishes (1974 figures)
figures from 'Let my People Grow'; David Wasdell, 1974

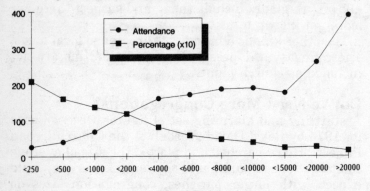

Size of Parish

is virtually invisible. The large parish is a mission disaster area. Its clergy are themselves buried under occasional offices. Its boundaries contain over 95% of unreached people, religiously protected from the gospel by the very boundary that was intended for their benefit. And certainly if it were to reach 10% of the people it would not have a building or staff capable of receiving them.

Since the time of Wasdell's survey, the tiny rural parish has rightly been eliminated, largely because of declining clergy numbers. But more parishes of modest size are needed, and more permissions to reach the groups of 3,000 to 5,000 people within larger parishes who are unchurched. A valuable goal would be a church for each micro-community of 2,000 people – more congregations, even if led by laity.

Three Chapters in Church Planting: Or, Three Stages in Planting History

Statistics can be misrepresented; but figure 5 is the least equivocal of all the charts. It divides into three chapters of church planting history. Starkly put, the first shows an average of one per year. The second, a rise to six per year, and then in the last six years (when church planting data has been more widely available), that growth has tripled to eighteen per year, or three every two months.

Figure 5

UK Anglican Plants 1967–1990

NB: Incomplete.   19 known plants being researched.

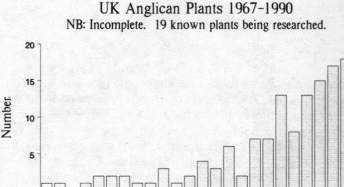

Moreover, these figures are out of date already. There are 19 further plants currently being researched. Only three years ago, the Church Planting Conference hoped that the Church of England might achieve one church plant per month. Now, in faith and some realism, the hope is one plant per fortnight.

If that seems audacious, it must be remembered that every year for the last 20 years, the Church of England has on average closed one church per week. There is a long way to go.

Is Big or Small Beautiful in Church Planting?

We know what size plants were when they began (see figure 6). These facts will help to break down the stereotype some have of church planting as charismatic imperialism or church plant invasion. The figure given is calculated by adding together the team taken with the residual congregation where one existed.

Seven out of ten plants begin with fewer than 25 people. Indeed, in the first ten years there was no other pattern. Big may or may not be beautiful; but it is not the norm.

Figure 6

Congregation Size at Start of Plant

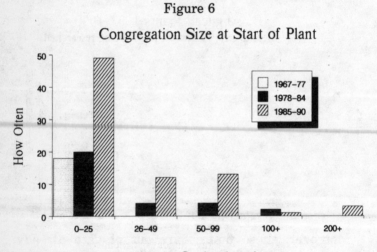

Average Sunday Attendance

The 1978–1984 period began to see changes during which a third of church plants started with larger groups, of up to a hundred or more. Plants were started not just by a seed team of one or two people, not even by a large house group, but by the transplant of an instant congregation – the 'from strength in strength' model.

The years 1985–1990 have repeated the patterns and proportions of 1978–1984. There is little evidence of a drift towards big church plants becoming the norm. They are just one helpful way, from existing large churches. Equally valid are the small beginnings characteristic of UPAs, new towns, and Local Authority estates, with pioneering work done by small, courageous teams. The challenges and pressures of each size are different, not better or worse. What counts is how they progress.

Healthy Plants Grow

Figure 7

Size of Attendance at Plants (March 1991)

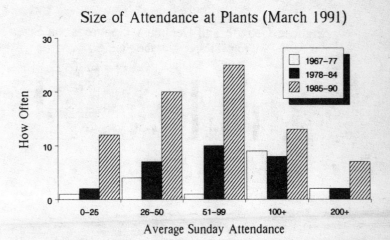

Comparing figures 6 and 7 shows that there are many healthy churches growing from modest beginnings. Only 7% of plants over five years old have remained under 25 for normal Sunday attendance. While under 25 is the typical start, growth to around 100 is the typical response. Overall figures for the period to date show that for every team member taken, three further members have subsequently joined a planted church.

Implications of Congregation Size

Concern with size is not to be dismissed as merely an unhealthy obsession with numerical growth. A survey undertaken by MARC Europe in 1989 suggests implications for the whole future of the congregation. For example, no churches under ten members grew at all, and all those over 400 reported growth.[4] MARC's research suggests that growth becomes common only when churches are larger than 50. Across the denominations, church planters on the ground report that 50 is the first major hurdle to cross. This observation is further confirmed by the numbers of static churches under that size.

Figure 8

Anglican Growth and Decline v Congregation Size
(From 'Prospects for the Nineties')

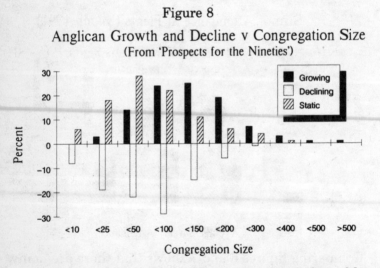

It is clear that smaller churches are most vulnerable to decline. The greatest decline was discovered in groups of less than 100 people. It was the awareness of this early vulnerability, the need to break through the barrier of 50, and the needs of full churches to export larger numbers of members, that has led to more larger groups being sent to plant. The unpalatable reality is that size is a significant factor. Increasing the number of permanently pygmy congregations must be avoided.

Transplants

The jargon of church planting is still settling down. Planting is a loose term, covering the range from the beginning of a congregation in virgin territory, to the relocation of part of a congregation in another church which is under threat of closure. We need to be more precise, and some of us in research talk of 'grafts' to mean a situation where the incoming team is smaller than the receiving group. We also talk of 'transplants', in two ways.

Figure 9

UK Anglican Plants – Grafts and Transplants 1967–90
from 'Prospects for the Nineties'

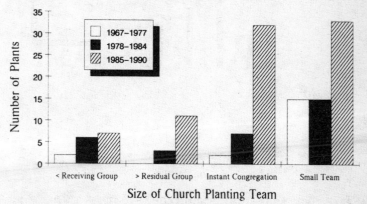

The first is where the incoming group are more numerous than a residual group, and by agreement are senior partners in the new venture. The second is when an instant congregation is transferred to a new location. In terms of group dynamics, instant congregation begins at around 20 people.

Grafts are a minority feature of the entire period surveyed. Transplants are also untypical, but becoming more frequent in the last five years. The most obvious change is in the proportion of instant congregations in church planting: nearly as many examples as of the small team.

The Typical Church Plant

If there is a typical plant, then it happened in the last five years, within the existing parish, using a rented building, and starting with fewer than 25 people. But it could be in any district and for a variety of motives.

Yet, the reality to grasp is that there are many models, shapes and sizes: a welcome reminder that God's creativity always shows variety, and Anglican church planting bears that hallmark.

CHAPTER FOURTEEN

Theological Training and Church Planting

David Gillett, Trinity College Bristol

Peter Wagner said on a recent visit to England that he believes that church planting has the most significant contribution to make to fulfilling the Great Commission. His studies showed that while growing very large churches was good, this could never be the main means of reaching a nation within our generation. This task would have to be fulfilled by the multiplication of a host of smaller churches. His deduction from these observations was that our great need was for church planters and leadership training for this missionary movement. If this is true, then his argument concluded that our greatest need of all was for trainers of church planters.

David Gillett has been well aware of the challenges of a mission emphasis to the training programme and establishments of our church. He has been the Principal of Trinity College Bristol since 1987 when Dr George Carey moved to become Bishop of Bath and Wells. Prior to that, David and his wife Valerie had lived in Luton where he was vicar of St Hughes, Lewsey. Before that he had been on the staff of St Johns Theological College in Nottingham.

David was one of the speakers at the previous national conference on church planting in May 1989. He recognises

*that church planting is one of the factors of church life that
is challenging both selection and training for ministry. He
concedes that traditional patterns have focused exclusively
on the pastor/teacher model and omitted the pioneer-evangel-
ist and church planter. David has commended the Baptists
at Spurgeon's College for being among the first to respond
to this with a parallel programme of recruitment, training
and instruction.*

*In this chapter, David explains that theological training
serves not only to prepare for the ministry needs of today's
church but also reflects on the theological implications of
movements in today's church – such as church planting.
Interestingly, this leads him to question the essence of Anglicanism, which is also one of the Archbishop's main points
in Part One. It may be both significant and healthy that
church planting highlights this question. David identifies
additional essential elements of Anglicanism to add to those
proposed by Dr George Carey. However, church planting may
further challenge us to ask questions like how unalterable is
the essence of Anglicanism if aspects do not conform to biblical ecclesiology, and how much flexibility should there be
in interpreting this essence of Anglicanism for each new
generation and cultural context. The Gospel and Culture
movement has already helped church planters not only to
examine the appropriate evangelism for each context – but
also to explore appropriate patterns of church life for express-
ing the gospel in each culture.*

We have an increasing number of students now study-
ing for ordained and lay ministry, who either come
with some recent experience of church planting, or
are eager to discover more about it. Clearly, church
planting is a major factor in the life and mission of
the church today. There are implications for those of
us involved in training men and women for the mission and ministry of today's church.

Ministerial Formation

What kind of ministerial formation is needed? First, we must prepare people for collaborative ministry. Church planting is based on teams, not lone rangers. If the one-man-band idea has manifestly failed in a more static view of church life, then it is even more inappropriate in a view of the church's mission which looks to increasing by division and growth of congregations. I also believe that ordinands and non-ordinands should be trained together. Lay men and women will be church planters, and will be helped by some ministerial training. There is a need for collaborative lay and ordained leadership, within church planting, so that both may play their distinctive roles, with a real appreciation of the place and significance of the other.

We must also train for flexible ministry. Situations vary, and one church plant may need very different approaches from a previous one in which the minister has been involved. Too often in the past, we have motivated people to enter ministry full of enthusiasm and ideas, which have often dwindled into an unimaginative approach after the first decade. The demands of mission today require ministers with a commitment to learning and growth that lasts for the whole of their ministry. Cramming facts will not produce this, however sound and biblical they may be. We must deal also with the areas of personal and spiritual growth, vision and motivation.

Much ministerial training has already been seeking to shift towards an emphasis on enabling and equipping ministry. New plants must not become clergy-dependent. Even more important, the minister must not become dependent on his/her new baby!

The great danger for pastors in new churches is that they develop eccentric and unchallenged spiritualities.

The great value of the Anglican church is its rich, broad spiritual tradition which both values the Scriptures and has developed a liturgical life providing both for the committed and for those on the fringes. We can train ministers to take hold of these resources.

The Advisory Board of Ministry mainly selects pastors and teachers; yet the ordained ministry must be seen more in terms of outreach. What of evangelists? Prophets? And people with an 'apostolic' ministry of church planting? These areas must be reflected in our training as well.

Training for Mission

In a sense the training establishments are a child of the church. This is true in the area of church planting: we depend on it actually happening in real life, so that we can learn from it, reflect on it, and evaluate it in the light of Scripture and the history of the church's mission. So we depend on students' experience in church planting before they enter college. We need to be able to give them placement experience, where they can be involved in church planting during their time at college, and we need training parishes where a newly-ordained deacon can go and learn the habits of church planting at the beginning of his or her ministry. This year, I believe there was only one training parish in England where a specific part of the curate's brief was to get involved in a church plant from the beginning, with a view to moving out with it in eighteen months time. More such training opportunities are needed, as often the deepest grooves are cut in one's ministerial development in the first few years after ordination.

We must also learn from what is happening around the world, in Latin America for example. Some of their insights are far more extensive than ours, and we may also benefit from the pitfalls which they have discovered.

Colleges must play their part in the major shift that is needed in the church's ministry. If selection processes are too heavily weighted towards pastoral ministry, then so is theological education. We have to educate, form and train for ministry with a clear mission focus and commitment. At Trinity we seek to do this with a central commitment to mission and religion, recognising that we now live in a multi-cultural, multi-religious society. Within the next few years, we may shift the emphasis of our course further, to see its total focus within mission. So for example, we need to continue to teach doctrine, but to do so in the context of the missionary task of the church, rather than in the abstract categories of historical theology.

This kind of remodelling of how one does theology is far more important and effective than just adding a new module on the latest evangelistic method within a course. I am not pleading for less theology: in fact, there is much in modern-day evangelical and charismatic circles that is severely weakened by a lack of theology, even in the area of church planting. I am committed to better theology, still as rigorous and as stretching, but relevant to the task of today's church and alive with a dynamic concern for mission.

We do have a special unit in our diploma and degree courses at Bristol on church growth and decline. For the last two years we have included material on church planting in this course. Among the students who did this unit recently, there was general agreement that church planting is part of the strategy of the moment. We are able to learn from students' own experience of church planting, and have had student evaluations of church plants in Hong Kong, Korea, Soweto in South Africa, Nottingham, Woking and

London. Each of these was judged an evangelistic success apart from the last two examples!

The Critical Role of Theological Education

By critical, I do not mean judgemental and negative, but I refer to the positive and necessary task of theological reflection. Biblical, theological, historical and strategic questions must be asked about any new development within the life and mission of the church. Understandably, much of what we hear about church planting comes from practitioners, who often do not stop to ask the theological questions. But they must be asked, if we are to avoid being interested merely in what works and in immediate short-term gains. I will suggest some of the important questions.

Are we learning the lessons from Wesley in the eighteenth century? He was very concerned to keep a breadth of spirituality within the compass of the new awakening; he also ignored parish boundaries at times. Does this foster the renewal of the church? What are the longer-term effects upon the whole Anglican denomination, and the missionary commitment of its clergy?

Some have argued that the Victorian church building programme had within it the seeds of decline.[1] Should not this give us caution about planting new buildings?

Are we planting churches with a commitment to an Anglican ecclesiology and an Anglican view of mission and evangelism? This is a particularly urgent question for evangelical Anglicans. In our enthusiasm for the planting of a new church, we can miss some of the riches that are part of the essence of our church and its mission. This is not only a matter of liturgy, or how much of it we use, although part of our Anglican definition concerns its rich liturgical resources. Are we in danger of losing the idea of a parish church: in other words, are we planting a new parish-type church; or an independent evangelical congregation? Is it for all the people in the area, whatever their personal commitment to Christ, or just for the committed Christians? Is the newly planted church in danger of losing the Anglican genius in mission, which includes without questions being asked, but which draws into faith and instructs the newcomer so that they enter into a clear commitment to Christ within their local church? Is not this the essence of Anglicanism, which we can too easily lose.

Are there reasons to keep to parish boundaries, even if this hinders a possible church plant? Do they not preserve something of lasting worth, which could easily be lost for a temporary gain? On the other hand, are there valid reasons (not only for the purposes of church planting) which require us to look again at the rigidity of parish boundaries and their negative effects in mission, without losing the positive benefits?

These are hard questions, and there will be others. They need to be asked by those of us committed to church planting as an important part of evangelism today; alternatively, they will become the ammunition of those who would oppose.

CHAPTER FIFTEEN

Preparing to Plant

Bob Hopkins and George Lings

I have introduced George Lings in Chapter 13. As an analyst and researcher he has picked up much valuable insight to help in the planning and preparation for a plant. My wife Mary and I received a specific call to be involved in church planting in England back in 1974. That led us to train for ordained ministry but to choose non-stipendiary licence so that being self-supported we could go where a parish would be unable to fund us.

It was not until 1983 that the opportunity arose for us to move out from our home church at Christ Church, Chorleywood. Then a door opened for us to leave the South East and go to Holy Trinity, Parr Mount in St Helens, Merseyside. We moved with three others to form a team of seven with the vicar Chris Woods and his wife, Kathy. This venture taught us key lessons for church planting, especially in the areas of team dynamics and a common vision, cross-cultural adaptation and appropriate evangelism and nurture for a UPA parish.

Having planted a local community church God led us to start a training programme for church planters. The pilot scheme was worked out with the Church Army and the on-going courses are run with Youth with a Mission at their Parr Mount Base in St Helens. Four annual schools have sent out pioneers into all sorts of situations up and down the country – about half of them Anglican. There are inter-national teachers at the forefront of church planting who visit this school and from whom we have learnt much.

It was in 1986 that I began to co-ordinate a network of Anglican leaders interested in church planting. From a small mailing list numbers grew to over 500 by 1989. As well as periodically circulating items of interest, the main focus has been organising annual day conferences in co-operation with Holy Trinity Brompton. From some 70 at the first event in 1987 we have grown to over 700 at the event which gave rise to this book. Throughout the years we have had committed support from some bishops, archdeacons, diocesan missioners, a theological college principal, many vicars and not a few parish groups and ordinands. Editing this book has been yet another opportunity to learn from the interaction between all contributors.

We have always sensed God's heart for unity in the mission ventures of church planting. Hence, when we heard of the DAWN (Discipling a Whole Nation) strategy of co-operative inter-church church planting and evangelisation, we sought to get involved. I am currently on the steering committee for the English DAWN-type initiative which goes under the name of Challenge 2000 (see Appendix A). It is our prayer that this will extend the opportunities for fruitful church planting and promote harmony in the Body of Christ.

In the last year God has put us in a growing team and has opened a number of opportunities for us to help parishes to review their mission plans and prepare for planting where appropriate. We have developed a series of training events and a parish weekend programme especially to help a whole church embrace the challenge of change associated with planting possibilities. It aims to inform, so as to dispel con-fusion and to clarify differing but equally valid callings for those who 'go' and those who 'stay'.

St Paul's Anytown PCC wanted to know where its members lived, so their homes were plotted on a blank map of the area. A dot represented a Christian family or an individual within a family. Adding the parish boundary threw light on the spread in the area. Most of the people at St Paul's lived within the parish, which was a comfort to the vicar, who was worried about what his neighbours thought. Yet still they lacked the information which would enable them to plan for the future.

Superimposing the railway line and the borders of a housing estate showed two possible challenges. The railway reached Anytown in 1884, serving the established community to the south and east. More dense, smaller housing was built north of the railway after its arrival. The two areas are socially different and geographically distinct. Access to the church is only through the one railway bridge. Yet a good number come to church through the work of a succession of curates whose house is north of the railway. St Paul's could plant a congregation into the community north of the railway, using the upper room at the pub, the Startled Saint.

There is an alternative. The vicar is also concerned that only two widows come to church from the notorious Green Bank housing estate. There could be a congregation started using the Green Bank community hall before the Sunday bingo session. How should they think about these two possibilities?

Progression and Pioneer Planting

The first of these ideas would be a *progression* plant. This is where churches have some strength of membership in a particular area or neighbourhood, or from a given social or cultural group. They build on this strength with a new congregation. The existing members become the nucleus for the new congregation, or the team members for starting the new church plant.

The second idea, by contrast, would be a *pioneer*

plant. This is where a church identifies a group of people among whom there are virtually no existing church members or attenders. This could be because there are social or ethnic barriers between the church and a particular housing estate or racial group. Alternatively, there may be no such differences, but merely a physical barrier, such as a motorway or railway, that blocks natural networks of relationship and community.

The challenges are greater for pioneer plants, since they are not building on a significant existing presence and witness of church members in the target area or group. However, if the barrier is just physical or geographic, then it may be overcome by some members relocating and making the right choice of a worship venue. But if the crossing of a social or ethnic barrier is involved, it will be vital to look for a team with cross-cultural gifting. Further, the team must not be too large, or it may either never adjust to the new situation, or will produce 'transplant rejection' by the host community.

Both progression and pioneer plants are valid tasks, but their difference is considerable. And to pioneer plant, churches need to learn the hard lessons of how to adapt to be church in ways appropriate to a different culture.

Culture

We know from Acts 10 how Peter's cultural prejudices needed to be overcome for him to reach the non-Jewish Cornelius. Another biblical example of Christians not being sensitive to culture was the Judaisers who plagued Paul on church planting journeys into Asia and Europe. The grace of the gospel is unique among world religions. Paul battled to keep us free to present the saving relationship with God through Jesus to any culture. People of that culture must be free to express that relationship in their own forms and patterns – that is one of the signs that the relationship with God is truly founded in grace and faith, not on law and works.

Christians in modern history have been little more aware of these principles than their New Testament counterparts, and often might be described as 'Gentilisers'. To arrive at cultural sensitivity, the humility to sit and listen is needed, rather than the common inclination to stand and talk.

Cultural difference is not just a matter of national or ethnic differences. Often, it is harder to see the cultural differences in our country that do not relate to these factors. Consider for example the differences between middle class surburbia in the south of England, and the urban industrial working class in the north. On one level, it is pie and peas rather than cheese and wine at church social events. But it also means tabloid and comic-strip nurture group material, rather than paperback books. Bible studies need to be developed that start from individual experiences and then look for biblical counterparts. The sermons need to be far more practical, with life-related stories free from conceptual and philosophical teaching. The home meetings, decision making, leadership patterns and outreach strategies, will need to be structured in ways appropriate to the culture.

God created cultural diversity to make beauty in variety. The Holy Spirit must be allowed to shape authentic worship responses that come from the heart of those he touches, in ways that are naturally and culturally appropriate for them.

We also need to examine our hearts and ask how to respond to smokers, beer drinkers, and the host of unmarried mothers and couples. We are challenged to distinguish between Christ's acceptance of all, and middle-class barriers and prejudices.

A contrast can be drawn between 'top-down' and 'bottom-up' approaches. The traditional top-down approaches have tended to be insensitive to cultural differences. This has colluded with our tendency to an evangelism which focuses on individuals, their personal response, and their assimilation into the existing church culture. Their group or family settings and norms get overlooked. Similarly, church planting plans have sometimes been motivated by a crude geographical examination of places and unreached areas, with little concern or awareness for the sorts of different people that make up the population there. This culturally insensitive evangelism and culturally inappropriate church planting will prove depressingly ineffective, or only recruit the compliant.

A rediscovery of a people-group approach is more aware. It will have a collective concern to develop ways of evangelism which will present the gospel in terms most readily received within the culture, and is addressed to meet the real areas of need. Church planting strategies will be implemented with models of church life which are truly indigenous and contextualised.

Alongside people-groups, whose identity is determined by ethnicity or language, it is important to consider socio-cultural groups, whose identity is determined by other factors. See some examples overleaf.

The twin objectives of mission must also be remembered. God has promised that he will bless all the nations, or people-groups, of the world through the church (Gen. 12:1–3). But he has also directed the church to remember the disadvantaged of society (Matt. 25:34ff.). Research into needs and opportunities must keep both these priorities in mind.

Socio-Cultural Factor	Examples
Occupation	Students; nurses; truck-driver
Residential class	Owner-occupied housing; bedsitters
Religion	Moslem; Hindu; Mormon
Education	Secondary school; university
Special needs	Alcoholics; prostitutes
Medical	Deaf; blind; disabled
Nationality	Dutch; Irish; American
Recreational	Rubgy players; bowlers
Stage of life	Young mothers; retired people

How can churches ensure appropriate mission strategies? Research and assessment is a key factor, which is why the concept of 'mission audit' or mission assessment programme (MAP) has been developed.

Mission Audit

This can broadly be described as strategic research and analysis. But it is helpful to consider the two parts of the name. 'Mission' means there is a defined task or objective. 'Audit' means to take stock, to examine in order to establish and confirm facts. So a mission audit is an investigation into a people, an area, a culture, or a neighbourhood, for the purpose of mission.

Mission audits as a formal procedure are relatively new, but are rapidly gaining in popularity, especially in the context of the Decade of Evangelism. Some dioceses are making them mandatory for all parishes. Resource packs are available to assist in the task.[1]

In mission audits, there are two main areas of focus.

The first is the community to be reached; and the second is the church, the body of believers, who are the resource for the mission task. These two areas will be looked at in turn.

Analysing the Community

Here, there are three components: to observe, converse, and research. Observation starts with a definition of the mission area, and understanding its relationship to the wider community of the town or city. For example, in one case it was the Four Acre Estate, which is set in an area of Sutton separated by a large park from the centre of St Helens. It was necessary to divide up the neighbourhood of some 2,000 homes into areas, each to be investigated by a pair of workers. They first walked around the area with prayer, seeking both to observe and to discern. The couples looked at the geography noting especially things like the natural barriers to community, such as railways, main roads and factories. They were also assessing social and economic factors, classifying the housing types and looking for the number of cars, telephones, queues at bus stops, and so forth. They also looked out for facilities and social meeting points, like health centres, shops, schools, pubs, and take-away food shops. They noted whether the houses and gardens or yards, and the streets themselves, were well cared for.

The second stage is conversation. It would be wrong just to look, and to stop there. Conversations both give information, and begin to build relationships. These can be chats with folk at the bus stop, street corner, or shopping centre. Door-to-door interviews are also helpful. There are a range of questionnaires available, and these can be designed as bridges to a developing ministry in the area. It is useful to talk to key community contacts in the neighbourhood, such as health visitors, shop owners, or community centre wardens.

These conversations will cover three aspects of community life:

1. *General information*: age, gender, children, marital status, vehicle ownership, employment and housing.

2. *Environment information*: services available, opinions of the area, friendships, perceived needs.

3. *Spiritual information*: affiliations, opinions, likes and dislikes, attendance at worship, knowledge, expectations.

The third stage is research, using resources from libraries or local authorities. This can provide valuable insights into the shared story of the neighbourhood, as well as demographic and sociological statistics. For example, area statistics concerning the environment, population, age range, marital status, and employment can be collected; along with historical information about the area. What is the general history? What incidents or tragedies have been significant? Has there been marked immigration or emigration of different groups? What is the history of the church or other religions in the area?

Analysing the Church

The other focus in a mission audit is the planting church itself. Some use the audit process to awaken the church to its mission task. Whatever approach is taken, here is an illustrative method of assessment divided into three parts.

First, the congregation. What are its likes and dislikes, opinions, its visions, plans and goals? What expectations does it have?

Next, the organisations in the church, such as home groups, mothers and toddlers groups, and so on. What is their function? How fruitful are they? How is their membership distributed across the whole church? What does the future look like?

Third, the statistics need attention. The profile of age, gender and marital status can be discovered; the attendance figures; seating capacity; finances; where new members are coming from; and other factual matters.

This analysis of the church is particularly relevant when assessing or planning a plant. Such simple things as the location of the members and of existing home groups are key factors, which could determine both *where* and *with whom* the plant should take place. The information gained about the gifting of the members and the evangelistic motivation of existing groups can also help to shape plans.

Preparing For a Church Plant: Forming a Team

Team size for a church plant is the first consideration, as each has its own characteristic strengths and weaknesses.[2] The smallest team of all is like a *lone seed* planted into a new area. This may be a couple, or the lone missionary at a pioneer plant. At this size there is no church meeting or worship to invite people to. Contacts are only made individually in the community, on doorsteps and in shops. Early meetings may take the form of evangelistic discussion groups in a home. It is essential that one or both members be gifted evangelists, and have a thick skin to endure the hard nature of the task, as well as the ability to persevere. Alternatively, the one or two may be a tiny graft slid into an existing group, the purpose being that they provide a breakthrough point in the community, or a leap forward in team relations, or a specialist skill in ministry.

Next comes the *small group*, perhaps between three and twelve people. When it is a team who relocates, then it is likely that the team dynamics will be close. Adversity brings people together. As a result, identification of gifts will be accelerated. The group is likely to find the mix of strategic gifts by necessity.

As we enlarge the planting unit we come to what we could call the *big house group* of thirteen to nineteen. In fact, this might well be one house group from the parish church, consisting of members who live in a specific area. The danger here is that mutual support remains the primary goal as many house group leaders have pastoral gifts. Through its size, the group feels secure, and sees less need to find evangelists among its members. The group will fill its house meeting, emotionally making little room for outsiders. However, at fewer than 20 people, it will be a bit small to take a community building. The way through these hazards lies in preparation, to gain vision for the area before being planted, and to discover evangelistic gifts. Once again evangelism may need to precede the start of public worship services.

With more than 20, the *mini congregation* begins. Like the other teams, it needs to identify evangelistic gifts, and also to grow together because it is probably a mix of more than one house group. In seeking premises it would look for those which allow growth without dwarfing the existing group. Examples might be a pub room, or a small school hall. It is large enough to start Sunday services, as well as offering mid-week meeting points appropriate to the culture.

Instant congregation is well under way at 50 or more. Having done some homework and publicity, it can start services right away and generally behave as a transplanted church. The blend of gifts is likely to be in place: if not, the planning has been poor. There is a danger that the community will think the new church needs nothing. People respect vulnerable ventures. There is also a danger that the new congregation will fail to adapt to the community around it.

What are the gifts needed on a team? The first requirement is evangelists. Pastoral gifts follow soon after, for the care of those who come and for the team itself. Some need to be gifted in the area of prayer and hearing God. A relaxed and flexible worship leader is important. Overall leadership will be needed as well. In a small church, the leader will be a specialist in one of these areas, and also a generalist who can hold the team together. This leader may be from the clergy or laity, as calling, gifting and availability are what count, not status.

Church life sometimes falls apart not for lack of ability, but for lack of maturity. People need gifts of 'being' as well as 'doing', so look for those with stickability. Often, a team has a breakthrough person who keeps going and sees long-term goals. Teams also need people who model interdependence. Paul and Barnabas are a biblical example. Lastly, no team can ever have too many encouragers. Paul frequently mentions Titus in his most troubled letter, 2 Corinthians.

All who go need vision. They must believe themselves called by God in order to stay the course. These calls need testing by the church, noting that gifts are not the sole criterion. A mix on the team of indigenous and itinerant can be a good balance. In a progression plant, more local people are needed; while in a pioneer plant, specific gifts are the key factors.

There are some who should *not* go. Staffing a church plant with those disaffected by the mother church is a mistake. Plants are not Siberian labour camps for parish dissidents! Those who transferred to the church because of dissatisfaction elsewhere will probably leave in the same way. People with a spirit of independence and who make bids for power are not suitable. The deeper one goes into mission, the more a servant attitude is needed. Jesus was the model missionary and servant.

Preparing For a Church Plant: Other Considerations

The location of the church plant building is critical. When shopping redevelopments are decided, location is the prime factor, as shops need to be where the people are. Churches are no different. They cannot be tucked away and thrive.

The building needs to be culturally warm, or at least neutral. Plants do not occur in police stations! If the culture is a mobile society, easy parking is important. If the stress is on family, then the location needs to allow family worship, a children's area, and an area to socialise. Practical details are important, such as the heating bill, or the lack of heating. The size of the building must match the size of the team – neither so big as to dwarf it, nor so small that it is nearly full to begin with. Moving takes energy and time and sets progress back.

As part of the preparation, planting bereavement must be taught. There are real losses to the church, and preparation will lessen the surprise, hurt, anger and bewilderment. There are also losses to those who leave, who will miss what they most valued of the previous ministry, whether that is the teaching, the music, the fellowship, or the pastoral care. They will miss seeing their friends and being in strong groups.

For those who stay, there are gains. They become a sending church; and Jesus said it was more blessed to give than to receive. The implication of Acts 13 is that if there is doubt, the best should be sent. Those who stay find they are remotivated for evangelism seeing empty pews and chairs. They are stirred to pray for local mission, to discover new gifts to fill the gaps, and to enjoy seeing fresh leaders and new Christians.

The team that goes needs support, but must also be allowed freedom. The aim is interdependence between sister churches. Resourcing can be a two-way street, and in one situation the planters came back to train, while the sending church released its most talented musicians to the plant.

There are problems with the satellite model: to remain in permanent orbit, always dependent, seems less than independent adulthood. It smacks of organisational necessity, not relational trust. If viability is the aim, the plant must be by stages supported, weaned and encouraged to establish its own separate identity, and finally taught to reproduce in turn. The sterile plant has limited viability indeed.

The Life Cycle of a Planting Church

Lastly, a helpful analogy is to think of church planting as a succession of stages in life: conception, pre-natal, birth, infancy, adolescence and maturity.[3] The next stage is further reproduction to complete the cycle. As in the life of a human body, viability centres on a successful conception, pregnancy, and safe delivery at birth. In this analogy, birth corresponds to the first public worship service, with all that precedes it going on behind the scenes.

Conception corresponds to defining the vision, giving it life in prayer, and identifying the core team to carry it forward. The team then begin with the strategic planning which develops from the mission audit. The plan will define the area and the timing. The team will expect God to direct them in these things, as also in the matter of appropriate outreach methods and the emerging philosophy of ministry and worship.

The *Pre-natal* phase can see the beginnings of evangelism flowing from the audit work and the training of the team. Looking for those who are open and responsive is the key, so as to build local people quickly into the growing team and disciple them into co-workers. Fellowship life will begin to occur, as relationships are cemented. Identification of gifts and the appointment of leaders will emerge.

Birth: to ensure a successful launch when the church plant goes public is vital. The timing must be right, neither premature nor overdue. We have already explained the importance of the right meeting place with appropriate facilities. Plans will have been laid for a worship team with leaders, musicians and arrangements for children according to resources. Linking with a major festival like Christmas or Easter gives an excellent opportunity for publicising the church planting event, and helping a high level of community interest and response.

In *infancy*, there is rapid growth, but instability as new people join. There is need for relationship building, communication of vision, leadership training, and small nurture groups. There is a danger of reaching a plateau here, with no further growth, unless there is a continuing emphasis on outreach. Infancy will develop into *adolescence*: this is the stage where the identity of the church is reassessed, with new vision and further planning. Property and buildings will be developed. The church will begin to achieve the full balance of church life and activities.

Maturity is characterised by stability in leadership

and a firm sense of identity. The church is self-governed and self-supporting. It must continue to be outward-looking and motivated for mission. It will be ready to complete the cycle by reproducing disciples, leaders, and new churches.

This life-cycle analogy will not fit every situation. But it provides a valuable model for healthy, continuing development of church planting initiatives.

CHAPTER SIXTEEN

Rural Church Planting

Chris Edmondson

Chris Edmondson is well qualified to discuss the challenges for church planting in rural England. He and his wife Susan gained first hand experience of an Anglican church plant when he was vicar of St George's Halifax. There he established a worship service in a community centre at the heart of a council estate.

This was an urban area, and Chris's knowledge of the rural context was acquired when he moved to be vicar of the village of Bampton in 1986 and to take the post of Officer for Evangelism for the Diocese of Carlisle. He has now had five years of wrestling with the quite different challenges of appropriate evangelism in village communities and ways of strengthening and multiplying rural church life.

Chris admits that most of the examples of rural church planting in England are not Anglican and they may often highlight the problems as much as the solutions. However he does point the way for us to suggest how principles of mission, multiplication and incarnation can be worked out in our more static and tightly-knit village communities.

Among these principles are the multiplication of church life 'in the small' to reflect the scale of rural life. Chris cites examples of new initiatives with small gatherings in outlying farmhouses and a barn. In the seminar at which he presented this paper, another story of an Anglican rural planting into a barn was recounted. It was undertaken by John Askey, the Anglo-Catholic vicar of Little Thetford in the Ely diocese for some seventeen years, who with the help of an independent evangelisation agency planned a mission to reach the many unchurched in his village. Appreciating the desire for continuing traditional worship patterns of the existing parish congregation, he deliberately planned to disciple the new converts from the mission in a church plant in a local barn. This has flourished; although the worship style is more modern, the church wardens and members of the original congregation have recognised the authentic work of God in the changed lives of the new group and have now invited them to establish their service back in the parish church building.

These developments give encouragement that the principles that Chris shares here can lead to new initiatives for mission and multiplication in the countryside which respect the quite different nature of the rural communities and express their life from within village culture.

Church Planting and the Rural Situation

The English Church Census of 1989, published in Spring 1991, shows that 160 new Anglican churches have been planted since 1975, one third of which continue to have significantly growing congregations. But are the models and examples from mainly urban and suburban areas relevant to rural communities? What church planting has there been in these areas?

Until the mid-eighties, there were hardly any examples (if any at all) within the Anglican church, although there were instances in other denominations. Barry Osborne, now director of 'Rural Sunrise', contacted fifteen churches which had been planted in rural areas, none of which were from the mainstream denominations. He observed two ways in which these plants had come about. One was when a group of enthusiastic Christians moved into a village, whose perception was that the established church presence lacked life. The second was when a town church locally sent some of its members to establish a Christian presence in a village. Two thirds of these fifteen plants were in the pentecostal, charismatic tradition; and one third in the independent, evangelical tradition.

These plants seem to have encountered a lot of problems. First, there was lack of leadership, often because the pioneer planter was not gifted in the ongoing work of building up a fellowship. Second, there were conflicts with established churches. Third, there were problems with premises. Fourth, there were problems about inconsistent support from worshippers, and fifth, there were some instances where the leadership was not local to the village which made establishing a church difficult. I mention these non Anglican plants, as the problems encountered are relevant to the Church of England situation as well.

Effective evangelism in the countryside will only come from those who understand and are committed to rural life. What are the characteristics of the rural scene?

1. Church attendance in Rural Areas

The Church of England has traditionally been considered strong in the countryside. The census mentioned above shows that it is indeed stronger than in the inner city and parts of suburbia, but nevertheless still in decline.

The main areas of growth seem to be the 'rural commuter areas', for example Buckinghamshire, Hampshire, Kent, and parts of the Midlands. The survey also shows growth in the Isle of Man and in Lincolnshire. In my own area of Cumbria, there was an overall decline in adult attendance of 3% among all denominations, but in the Church of England an increase of 3%, between 1985 and 1989. In 1989, church attendance represented 14% of adults and 9% of the child population.

Although there is relative strength in rural areas, this is no cause for complacency, and new strategies for future growth are needed.

2. The Integrity of the Rural Church

The rural church is not simply a smaller version of the urban church. The picture of the 'successful' urban or suburban church will be different from that found in the countryside. A rural church with fifteen or twenty people as regular worshippers is not 'failing' because it lacks the resources of a larger urban church.

3. Perceptions of the Church

The distinctions between church and community are much more blurred in rural areas. If the model of the church is that of the communal, all inclusive parish church, then any sort of church plant might seem almost like treason. Alternatively, if the model is more of the associational, gathered church, then there would appear to be more scope for church planting.[1] The ecclesiology needs to be thought through before any venture is undertaken.

4. Different kinds of 'Rural'

Bishop Anthony Russell has suggested that there are essentially four countrysides. There is the Urban Shadow, the Accessible Countryside, the Less Accessible Countryside, and the Remote or Marginal Countryside.[2] Evidence suggests that the rural commuter areas, which are often in the Urban Shadow category, offer more possibilities for developments in church planting than do the smaller, more remote communities. This is to do with culture as well as size:

the rural commuter areas have more of a suburban culture, while in the remote areas the traditional pattern of rural life has been less obviously affected.

5. Survival

In many rural communities the main concern is to survive, not to grow. In my own village, the population is declining, making this even more prominent an issue. Another factor is that the village church must serve all the people: there is no option to choose a particular style of church. This raises the issue of how that Christian community can be distinctive without being exclusive, a question which can put great pressure on the leadership and membership of the church. There is also the matter of coping with old, large buildings. The 1989 English Church Census revealed that 53% of church buildings are more than 500 years old, and many of these are in rural communities. The church building as a place is of greater importance than in a town. To quote *Faith in the Countryside* (1990):

> It is a totem, a focus of identity even to those who hardly ever cross its threshold ... even those who may feel indifferent to the Christian religion will often support fund raising to carry out an important repair to the parish church.[3]

Thus, a small group of people faced with a £1,000,000 repair to their building (as a church in Devon is facing); or in my own diocese the need for £180,000 to repair a church roof where the population in just 800, make it difficult for people to think about growth and evangelism. They are simply trying to maintain a Christian presence recognising the importance of the church building in this task.

The Task

The first priority is to help the leadership of the church and its members to see the importance of what God is already doing and saying in the situation, and to seek to cooperate with that.[4] Listening – to God, to individuals, to the community as a whole – is vital. The history of the community must be acknowledged. The 'Mission Audit' process in an appropriate form may be helpful in discovering whether a church plant might be the right way forward.

One relevant model is that discussed by Neil Weston and David Bourne in *Taking on Faith in the Countryside* (1991).[5] This is the 'Minster' model, in which a larger church in a given area will serve satellite churches in the surrounding district. Each will preserve its own identity, but will be served from the centre, in the same way as some models of church planting.

The rural church needs to believe in itself and the power of God again. There are many dispirited, small congregations who have ceased to believe in God or in themselves. That is the starting point in many areas. Innovation is often the key to reversing the decline. For example, there is a parish in Cumbria where the church is in the middle of a field two miles from the nearest house. This is not a recipe for church growth and they may need help in considering using the school, in the centre of the community, as an alternative or additional place for worship. This work in changing perceptions is a long-term process, but may be the key to long-term growth.

Even when a church has been declared redundant, it is still possible to hold a certain number of services in the building through the course of a year, without any financial outlay from the community. One parish in Cumbria which has a 'redundant' church is using it for special events and activities, drawing people from the three parishes for which the vicar is concerned. In the same area, a 'church in the barn' has been established, actually an offshoot of the Elim church in Carlisle, but established with the goodwill of the other local Christian communities.

Another group of Cumbrian churches did not set up a permanent church plant, but instead abandoned their evening service with dwindling numbers in a large building, and went round each Sunday evening to different farmhouses in outlying parts of the community. This proved effective in building up the existing fellowship of the church, and as a mean of evangelism and growth.

Conclusion

Most rural churches are not in the situation of some of the large urban churches looking to take over buildings to make room for expanding congregations! In my own village at Bampton, we could fit virtually the whole population of the parish into the parish church. Instead, what is needed is a vision for the countryside, credible leadership with the capacity to enable others, and deanery and diocesan structures prepared to take a radical look at their priorities.

CHAPTER SEVENTEEN

The Origin and Future of Parish Structures

Both David Pytches and Brian Skinner have served as bishops in the Anglican Communion in Latin America. David Pytches was specifically appointed Bishop of Chile, Bolivia and Peru because of his first-hand experience of church planting in that continent. Both bishops returned to England at different points to become vicar and curate team at St Andrew's Chorleywood.

Having seen growth to a congregation of over 700 they felt God directing them to explore planting initiatives from this powerful base. They have planted two congregations within the parish. One is geared principally to serve a council estate area which had previously been little reached. This team is led by the deacon, Margaret Knight. The second plant was focused on an area which is more representative of the majority, upper-middle class neighbourhood of the parish. This team has been led by two NSM curates, Jim Sutton and Bob Maynard. Both have full-time jobs in London. However, as has been explained in other contributions to this book (especially Chapter 13), planting tends to lead to more growth and hence creates further energy for more plants. This then inevitably confronts the problem of the parish boundary.

Having struggled, dialogued and researched for several years over how to move forward and remain true to their Anglican convictions, David and Brian wrote New Wineskins *in 1990. This proposes some ways forward to create greater flexibility for planting initiatives so that the momentum for mission is not stifled. In this final chapter they do not reproduce this material; rather, David presents some additional historical reflections on the origins of the parish system. Further research and dialogue has also shaped Brian's proposals, which again complement and add to their earlier work.*

I: Reflecting on the Origins of the Parish System

David Pytches

The traditional church in England has been divided into dioceses since the seventh century, with an adapted transplant of the administrative division of the Roman empire. Theodore of Tarsus, the Archbishop of Canterbury (668–690) divided England in such a way that he formed dioceses out of the existing kingdoms, or where they were too large, their tribal subdivisions. The division of dioceses into parishes with boundaries came later.[1]

Within each diocese, the work of the church was carried on from mission stations called minsters. These owed their foundation to a king or an important monastery (the Latin for a minster is *monasterium*). Minsters were not necessarily staffed by monks, but could also be staffed by secular clerics. The head of the minster was known as an 'abbas' or a 'praepositus', although these titles were not reserved exclusively for heads of minsters: they were applied to some other senior clergy also. The minster was often the bishop's headquarters, and served as a focal point for daily offices and training. The minsters also sent out teams to the villages, where they evangelised, baptised, and preached in the open air.

The word 'parish' derives from the Latin *parochia*, and has been used by the church since its very early days to denote the primary unit through which it carries on its mission. The ecclesiastical concept of a parish in those days differed considerably from the later medieval and modern institution of the same name. It meant a community of Christians in a city or a rural area, not a defined geographical region.

Tithing – the giving of a tenth of a person's income – had never been obligatory upon the community until 765 when it was enforced (in a circular letter to the bishops) by Pepin the Short (the father of Charlemagne) throughout the dominions, in order to finance the church. It was this which eventually led to the delineation of actual parish boundaries some 300 years later. A parish came to consist of the sum total of the lands from which the local church received its tithe.

The new practice of defining boundaries came about at this period of secularisation of the parish system. The process, however, led to ecclesiastical confusion. In some cases priests began inheriting their office from their fathers. In other cases, the revenues of many churches became enmeshed with the feudal system, and laymen were distributing only a fraction of the tithe to the church.

The most convenient point from which to trace the development of the parochial system in Anglo-Saxon England is the Domesday Book (1086), which shows that over large parts of England the old minster system had been replaced by the new parochial structure. The church's pastoral care was now exercised through small rural and urban units, each church with an endowment and its own priest.

The establishment of village churches had begun in earnest in the ninth century, but the large majority of the old parish churches in England were founded in the tenth and eleventh centuries. In the villages, the initiative for building churches came from the 'thane' who owned the village, or – as often happened in Danish England – from a group amongst the free elements in the population.

The organisation of parishes into rural deaneries and archdeaconries was not apparently complete until 1108. But claims for exceptions were advanced, and allowances made for churches classified as 'peculiars' – privately owned churches which usually pertained to royalty or the lord of the manor upon whose land they stood, and whose ancestors had built them. They had by nature been independent and continued to be free of the parish structure. Their incumbents were a kind of vassal to their temporal lord, holding office in return for service. One surviving example of such a 'peculiar' may be found at Calke in Derby. Similarly, there were monastic congregations which maintained independence.[2]

During the millennium since the creation of the parish boundary system in England, it has come to be seen as integral to the life of the parish church. Some would see it as almost essential. However, this has not been the case for much of the wider Anglican Communion. There is also some change beginning to take place in parts of the Church of England today. Peter Nott, the Bishop of Norwich, has made some apt observations. He writes:

If the interests of mission are to have priority, then

we must be prepared to be unsentimental about . . .
boundaries. These are matters upon which feelings
often run high, and in which we spend a great deal
of time and energy in debate and argument. Boundaries are very secondary considerations, and should
be dealt with decisively and without too much
wasteful debate.[3]

The former Archbishop of York, Lord Stuart Blanch,
cites and then comments upon the resolution of the
most recent Lambeth Conference, passed in full session:

This conference:
1) Calls for a shift to a dynamic missionary emphasis, going beyond care and nurture to proclamation and service.

2) Accepts the challenges this presents to the
   diocesan and local church structures and patterns of worship and ministry, and looks to God
   for a fresh movement of the Spirit in prayer,
   outgoing love and evangelism in obedience to
   our Lord's command.

Lord Blanch comments:

. . . This is well said, and it is encouraging to hear
that steps have already been taken to express that
full resolution in practice, for the church which is
not taking the Gospel to others is not true to itself.
That aphorism is pertinently illustrated in the history of Judaism. As the institution grew stronger
and the hierarchy more central to its life, the title
deeds of Judaism originally entrusted to Abraham
('In thee shall all the nations be blessed' – Gen.
12:3) were honoured more in the breach than in the

fulfilment. The nation which was called to be 'a light to the Gentiles' became increasingly preoccupied with keeping its own candle alight. There were prophetic voices raised against the process.

The Church, likewise, has often retreated from active mission to the world behind the bulwarks of the great institutions it has created . . . it could be that the episcopate of the future will have to exercise their apostolic task in ways more consistent with the ideals and methods of the apostolic church.[4]

Parishes with their boundaries seem so neat and tidy for diocesan administration. The system has been idealised as pre-eminently suitable for the care and conversion of souls. There is some truth in this, in that it serves well for pastoral care when there is a fair-sized congregation, but this is rare today. According to the latest statistics produced by MARC Europe, traditional churches between them are currently haemorrhaging some 50,000 souls a year, which is almost 1,000 per week. The biggest decline is in the Church of England, which is losing some 300 a week, equivalent to four local churches! Most of those lost are under the age of 30.[5] So plainly, as far as mission is concerned, the facts are quite the reverse from the idealised representation. Parish boundaries actually inhibit spontaneous evangelism and church growth. Those churches which know how to evangelise, in the sense of adding to the church, are limited to their own patch; whilst others who have dwindling congregations can resist any evangelistic enterprise of the Anglican church from any other parish.

According to Canon John Tiller:

The parochial system should be about the living witness of the local church, and not about defining 'cures for souls' for individual clergymen, who then become entrenched behind boundaries, where they are secure in their rights to operate a spiritual 'closed shop' as far as the Church of England is concerned.[6]

What is being said over and over again is that the model of a church with parish boundaries is too static and hinders normal spontaneous growth for many active churches today. The dynamic for church planting of any kind is too precious to quench lightly. It is the sovereign wind of the Spirit blowing. The scandal of wind is that it does not necessarily observe boundaries of any kind. The work of the Holy Spirit in building Christ's church is not only dynamic, but organic: church growth cannot be brought about simply by our planning or the endeavours of church bureaucrats. We must follow where we believe the Holy Spirit is leading. We cannot restrain him and restrict him by parish boundaries.

Whilst not necessarily rejecting the parish system *in toto*, the plea is for a greater degree of flexibility within the structure. There is precedent within the history of the church itself to give encouragement and point to a way forward. The bishops could revive alternative models, to act in parallel under their oversight. Elsewhere I have described a number of proprietary chapels which exist, and fall into precisely this category.[7] The church already operates with parallel spiritualities, parallel theologies, and parallel concepts of the ordained ministry. It should not be difficult to encourage the continuation and development of parallel structures within the Church of England.

The strong words which Jesus, the Lord of the Church, once said about the impossibility of bottling new wine into old wineskins (Luke 5:37–39), are still relevant today. We have rationalised away those words spoken nearly 2,000 years ago, and we can still ignore them at our peril. If we act on them, however, we shall discover a dynamic which has been missing in the life of our churches for far too long. Jesus is not saying we must destroy the old wineskin, nor does he condemn the old wine. He seems to commend it. If we do not listen to what he is saying here, the new will destroy the old and both will be lost. Is there anything more persuasive than that?

II: Alternative Structures for Planting

Brian Skinner

What ways can be found for Anglicans to plant churches beyond the boundaries of the initiating parish? While there may be many challenges to church planting within parish limits, it is also true that for many churches which are actively growing the most appropriate context for further extension is in areas beyond the parish. This may be either because planting has already been pursued successfully within the parish, or because growing churches are often increasingly eclectic. It is here that one experiences the most unhelpful anachronisms of the parish system. The ideal of local church allegiance is presumed in the concept of parish churches, but it is also taken for granted that Anglicans can travel to a neighbouring parish church if they feel the style, churchmanship or ministry of their own local church is unhelpful to them.

It is widely accepted that there needs to be a new emphasis in the church on growth, evangelism and mission. All the arguments in favour of church planting as a most effective means of evangelism and church growth do not need to be repeated here. However, they are just as relevant to the opportunities beyond the parish as within it.

The challenge to mission and growth in this Decade of Evangelism applies nationwide. In any case, Christ's commission to the world stands in its own right, irrespective of any special 'Decade'. The only argument which could carry any weight, in limiting one's vision to a particular area, is that all other areas were fully and effectively evangelised. But reports and statistics make it quite clear that this is not the case. I am not suggesting that churches in a given area are failing to preach the gospel. I do suggest that Jesus' statement is still true: 'The harvest is plentiful but the workers are few' (Matt. 9:37). I would also suggest that no one method, style or congregation is likely to be adequate to reach all those in any given area.

We have to acknowledge that the Church of England is not generally being very effective in reaching our nation for Christ. Many churches are not growing. Where a particular parish church, for whatever reason, is failing to make much impact, the parish system tends to protect that area from other neighbouring churches. This cannot be good as a strategy for evangelism.

The Real Nature of the Problem

My background is that of missionary work within the Anglican Communion. I have found it hard to understand the reasons against the growth and multiplication of the church through church planting, even when it is beyond the parish boundary. I have enquired of people, clergy and others, in order to clarify the arguments against, and weigh them against the Dominical commission to go into all the world.

The reasons can be summarised as follows:

1. The parish system traditionally understood is well

suited to mission and outreach throughout the country.

2. Observing parish boundaries promotes the unity of the church, both the Anglican church and the wider church.

3. Tradition, order and authority should be respected.

4. The rights of local clergy should be respected. The presence of other growing congregations can be threatening.

5. Competition within the church is unnecessary, unjustified, and ungentlemanly. To church plant within another parish is to imply that those already there are failing in their responsibilities.

6. Bishops are concerned for clergy within their care, not to allow them to be hurt, threatened or discouraged.

7. Bishops are concerned to maintain order, and not to approve something new, unusual or different without the official support of other bishops.

All of these call for honest evaluation, and provide warnings and challenges about the ways in which progress should be made. New things should not be sought for their own sake. However, time and circumstances change, and there are some ways in which the church needs to adapt in order to be more effective in preaching the gospel.

The parish system has played an important role in the life of the nation over the centuries, but now it is not an effective instrument for mission. By nature, it is well suited to pastoral oversight and meeting the needs of the flock, not bringing in the harvest.

These are times of variety in style, taste and expectation, because of the influence of various subcultures and the rise of individualism. The church needs to reflect this multiplicity in its expression of church life. It is not a matter of competition, but of complementary support, where the concern is for the whole church and not for isolated or individual enterprises. Unity is seen in our attitude to each other, not in our uniformity.

What gives me most concern is the defensiveness and possessiveness shown by many clergy. It is far more important to be in the place where God would have us, than to covet the 'success' of others. It seems tragic that so many clergy find their sense of security so strongly vested in their ministry, when we are those who teach the basic need for security and sense of worth to be found in Christ. Our greatest delight should be to see his will fulfilled, not our own achievements acknowledged. There may be many ways in which the gospel is presented, which we feel are less than the best, but no-one's ideal is best suited to everybody. Surely, variety and multiplicity are likely to increase the scope of overall outreach. Endeavours which could be seen as complimentary are too readily represented as objectionable, even when a greater number of people are being reached for Christ.

Possible Ways Forward

One way in which churches have been formed across boundaries is by the splitting off of house churches, either voluntarily or otherwise. This has many inherent problems. As Anglicans, we can learn from the house church movement of the past 20 to 30 years, profit from its strengths, and find ways of avoiding its most obvious pitfalls. We should not seek to perpetuate this pattern of growth.

If authorities and other colleagues are highly resistant to any variation from traditional patterns, the only viable option in some cases may be a kind of new-style house church. Such a church would look to the church which brought it into being for direction and oversight, but in other respects would not be regarded as Anglican. It may be that some arrangement of this kind could be adopted as a holding operation, in the hope that changes in Anglican rigidity are sufficiently near for this to be temporary. However, history suggests that once a break has been made, it is very difficult to bridge the gap and restore union, as with the Methodist Church.

Some incumbents may agree to allow a new church to develop in their parishes under their ultimate responsibility, without stifling their development. This is a lot to expect, but a worthwhile goal.

The favoured solution is that of parallel structures. This is the plea David Pytches and myself make in the book *New Wineskins* (1991). It seems entirely appropriate and fruitful. It does call for positive support from the diocesan bishop, and requires a good deal of publicity before it is likely to get established and recognised. Provided that due attention is paid to relations with other clergy and churches, this is the pattern most likely to encourage the spontaneous expansion of the church. It is most in line with New Testament accounts of the early church. It focuses more on life than on order; but that is no reason to neglect history's lesson about church structure. Flexibility need not mean chaos, and life and growth need to take precedence over rules and structures.

Issues to be Faced

There is a great need for debate and reflection. The real issues need to be brought into the open. There are many presuppositions which cannot stand up to reasoned argument, but will remain in people's minds unless challenged and discussed. Why should the fact of being an established church mean that the opportunities for growth and multiplication are so much more restricted for Anglicans than for the Free Churches? Why should the comprehensiveness of the Anglican church not be expressed in variety within an area, rather than in the huge differences between one parish and another? Why must something which was appropriate in the past remain unchanged and unchallenged in the present, when circumstances have changed?

These things need talking through at all levels. Arguments on both sides need weighing. Reflection is part of this process as well, as there are aspects of theology which need to be challenged. Church life is affected by things such as greater mobility, information technology, new attitudes to unity, increased individualism, attitudes to authority, and new educational methods. Not all these changes are welcome, but all must be part of our reflection.

First, there are issues of ecclesiology. Our understanding of the church must not be circumscribed by denominational allegiance. Due allowance must be given to the fact of multiple denominations working with their own authority structures, often without much consultation, yet nevertheless as part of the whole church. Authority needs to be rethought. Is Christian authority based on the determination of the State, or God's anointing? How is it recognised? How should it be exercised? What sanctions are appropriate, and is the concept of ecclesiastical courts still relevant?

Pastoral matters also need consideration. It does matter if fellow clergy are hurt or threatened. This does not mean that this risk should inhibit all progressive plans, but care must be taken to avoid unnecessary hurt, to repair damage done unwittingly, and to improve communication and consultation. A policy needs to be followed regarding the transference of membership from one congregation to another. The freedom of individuals to do this must be respected, but good communication and mutual respect can be promoted.

Church growth is a neglected area for Anglicans, partly because we tend to focus on growth as meaning larger church attendance and bigger collections. There are extensive studies showing the importance of how people relate to each other, and how they share things, and how change can be encouraged.

The Essence of Anglicanism

What makes a church 'Anglican', or is essential to Anglicanism? Whatever different approaches there may be to these questions, the Lambeth bishops have given a helpful start in their Lambeth Quadrilateral (1888). The preconditions of unity 'as Anglicans see them' are expressed as the acceptance of the Scriptures, the creeds, the two sacraments of baptism and holy communion, and the concept of episcopacy ('locally adapted') as an acceptable form of church government.[8] This is a broad enough definition to encompass flexibility over church planting, unless the understanding of episcopal government is restricted to some particular model.

One approach is to look at existing traditions, and to state that only that which fits within this can be regarded as Anglican. The problem with this is that there are already so many precedents and anomalies which exist or have existed in churches that are part of the Church of England.

The other approach is to focus on origin. If something comes from an Anglican source, and remains in fellowship or 'in communion' with the Anglican church, then it is Anglican (in much the same way as children born within a family belong to that family). There are two ways in which any group may cease to remain in communion with the Anglican church. One is for it to opt out, and choose no longer to be regarded as Anglican. The other is for it to be rejected and excluded from the Anglican church, by the bishop or by the synod. In this latter case, the reasons must be clear and justified; and it is doubtful that a simple appeal to tradition is adequate while *semper reformanda* remains a hallmark of the Anglican church. To appeal instead to ecclesiastical or even national law only highlights the fact that changes are needed at that level, when such law restricts the relevance and growth of the church.

The matter of episcopal oversight needs consideration. Legitimate authority must have its proper place, but this does not mean complete agreement with the views of any one bishop, or even agreement with the bishops as a whole. Respect for those in authority is a clear biblical injunction, but obedience will always be within the limits of conscience and in line with biblical values for church life.

Conclusion

We are committed to love and respect others, even when we hold different convictions about the way in which things are best done. This is the spirit which unites many existing Anglican churches, and this is the sort of relationship which could reasonably exist within parishes, if the concept of parallel Anglican

expressions were permitted within the overall jurisdiction of the bishop.

APPENDICES

Appendix A

DAWN: Discipling a Whole Nation

DAWN started in 1974 in the Philippines; but it was at the Lausanne II conference in 1989 that it made wide international impact. C. Peter Wagner has described DAWN as 'the most effective delivery system'[1] for helping the church complete the Great Commission. In countries where a national programme is fully under way, some very encouraging things are reported.

DAWN is not an organisation in itself, but a strategy adaptable to each national context. The full story is written in a book by Jim Montgomery, *DAWN 2000* (1991). A DAWN programme starts with accurate research on a nation (like a national mission audit), and in the case of England, this has already partly been done in the form of the MARC Europe English Church Census. From these accurate facts, every denomination is encouraged to set realistic goals for church planting and evangelism. Experience has shown that to give everyone an opportunity to hear the gospel and to see it lived out in a local body, one church for every 750 to 1,500 people is needed: that is, one per neighbourhood. The body of Christ is then mobilised in prayer and action, and the progress of plans is regularly reviewed.

In England, an initial consultation was held in March with some seventy church leaders. C. Peter Wagner is booked to give the main papers at a national congress in Birmingham, in February 1992, to launch such an initiative as part of the overall plans for the Decade of Evangelism.

The essence of the strategy is that realistic goals are set, based on real information and the corporate seeking of God, by a broad cross-section of the body of Christ.

Code of Practice – Ten Principles for Church Planting

In nations where co-operative, inter-church programmes of evangelisation and church planting have been developed, a statement of practice has sometimes been used to provide helpful guidelines. The shared task of discipling the nation was understood to involve the establishing of at least one church in every neighbourhood. A viable church for these purposes was a local group of believers associated for worship, instruction, fellowship, service and outreach, and who regularly keep the ordinances. These are the ten principles.

1. *Responsible Pluralism.* A given area or locality may have more than one group ministering in it.

2. *Mutual Respect.* A participating body, considering the possibility of entering a locality where there are existing churches, will consult with those churches with an attitude of respect.

3. *Proximity and Density.* When a new group enters a locality, it will evaluate and minimise any possible adverse effects due to proximity to an existing group. A dense population may reasonably allow different groups to be closer together than in sparsely populated areas.

4. *Unity with Diversity.* There is intrinsic oneness in the Body of Christ in the spiritual sense, and also due to the unity of the Holy Spirit. This does not mean that every part is the same. There is legitimacy for diverse structural and doctrinal distinctives within the organisations, groups and churches that co-operate together, and respect for individual sovereignty under God.

5. *Team Spirit and Fellowship.* Workers from different participating bodies working in a given locality are encouraged to arrange for communication and fellowship with one another to build a team spirit.

6. *Sharing Resources.* Each participating body in a given

locality is encouraged to make available its resources of personnel, finances and equipment, for the purposes of supporting evangelism and church planting efforts.

7. *Reaching the Unreached*. Participating bodies are encouraged to give priority to areas or groups where there is no resident gospel witness or church.

8. *Reconciliation*. Every effort should be made to resolve conflicts between participating bodies consistent with Matthew 18:15–17 and 1 Corinthians 6:1–8. Only when local efforts have been exhausted without success should a conflict be referred to a special Reconciliation Council of leaders from participating bodies.

9. *Church and Para-church Relationships*. The centrality of local church life is emphasised, and the supportive ministry of para-church groups recognised. Mutual respect and sensitivity is essential. Para-church organisations are encouraged to consult prior to developing plans for a given area.

10. *Common Planning*. Common planning among participating bodies should be done every two to three years, and each participant's plans shared.

Appendix B

Mission Audit Resources

Mission Assessment Programme (MAP) – Liverpool
Diocesan BMU
Contact: Captain Ken Gaskell (Diocesan Evangelist)
            1 Fairfield Road
            Dentons Green
            St Helens
            WA10 6AJ

            Tel. 0744 21505

Parish Audit and Profile – GUML (Group for Urban
Ministry and Leadership)
Contact: GUML Office
            St Bride's Church
            PO Box 82
            Liverpool
            L69 8AN

            Tel. 051 709 1463

Going for Growth – Liverpool Diocesan Resource Officers
Contact: Resource Officers
            Church House
            1 Hanover St
            Liverpool
            L1 3DW

Faith in the City: An Audit for the Local Church
Contact: Church House Bookshop
              Great Smith St
              London
              SW1P 3WZ

Mission Pursuit – United Reform Church
Contact: URC Supplies
              86 Tavistock Place
              London
              WC1H 9RT

Action in Mission (AIM) – Baptist Union
Contact: Baptist House
              PO Box 44
              129 Broadway
              Didcot
              Oxon
              OX11 8RT

An Introduction to Parish Audit
Action Speaks Louder (Handbook for Social
Ministry) – Liverpool Catholic Diocese
Contact: Pastoral Formation Team
              Curial Offices
              152 Brownlow Hill
              Liverpool
              L3 5RQ

Church Audit: Switching the Style – EUTP
Contact: Evangelical Training Project
              St Bride's Church Centre
              PO Box 83
              Liverpool
              L69 8AN

District Strategy: An Environment for Growth and Multiplication

Contact: St Helens Inter-Church Neighbourhood
Evangelism (SHINE)
Parr Mount School
Sorogold St
St Helens
WA9 1AX

Tel. 0744 24786

Bibliography

Addleshaw, G. W. O., *The Beginnings of the Parochial System* (Ecclesiological Society, 1986).

Addleshaw, G. W. O., *The Development of the Parochial System* (Ecclesiological Society, 1986).

Barlow, Frank, *The English Church 1066–1154* (Longman, 1979).

Blanch, Stuart, *Future Patterns of Episcopacy* (Latimer House, 1991).

Breen, Mike, *Growing the Smaller Church* (CPAS/Harper-Collins, 1992).

Brierley, Peter W., *Christian England* (MARC Europe, 1991).

Bunting, Ian, *Claiming the Urban Village* (Grove Books, 1989).

Cleverly, Charlie, *Church Planting – Our Future Hope* (Scripture Union, 1991).

Finney, John, and Lawson, Felicity, *Saints Alive* (Anglican Renewal Ministries, 3rd edn 1990).

Hill, Monica, *How to Plant Churches* (MARC Europe, 1984).

Holloway, David, *Ready Steady, Grow* (Kingsway, 1989).

Holt, Peter, *Moving Forward: A Strategy for the Diocese of Norwich* (1989).

Hopkins, Bob, *Church Planting: 1. Models for Mission in the Church of England* (Grove Books, 1988).

Hopkins, Bob, *Church Planting: 2. Some Experiences and Challenges* (Grove Books, 1989).

Montgomery, Jim, *DAWN 2000* (Highland Books, 1991).

Patrick, Bruce, *The Life Cycle of the Reproducing Church* (New Zealand Baptist Home Mission Board, 1990).

Pytches, David, and Skinner, Brian, *New Wineskins* (Eagle, 1991).

Tiller, John, *A Strategy for the Church's Ministry* (ACCM, 1983).

Wagner, C. Peter, *Church Planting – Keep to the Harvest* (Kingsway, 1991).

Warren, Robert, *In the Crucible* (Highland Books, 1989).

Warren, Robert, *On the Anvil* (Highland Books, 1990).

Weston, Neil (ed.), *Taking on Faith in the Countryside* (Grove Books, 1991).

Faith in the Countryside (Church House, 1990).

Lambeth Report (Anglican Consultative Council, 1988).

Notes

Introduction

1. *CPAS* paper 282, pp. 3–4.
2. *Renewal Magazine*, March 1991, pp. 27–8.

Chapter 1

1. *The Times*, London, Monday 13 May, 1991, Christianity without miracles?
2. Michael Nazir Ali, *From Everywhere to Everywhere* (Collins Flame, London, 1991), p. 67.

Chapter 2

1. See Michael Wooderson, *Goods News Down the Street* (Grove Books, 1982); and Michael Wooderson, *The Church Down Our Street* (Monarch, 1989).

Chapter 10

1. Mike Breen, *Growing the Smaller Church* (CPAS/Harper Collins, to be published early 1992).

Chapter 12

1. For a fuller account of the Chester-le-Street story, see Eddie Gibbs, *Ten Growing Churches* (MARC Europe,

1984) and David Pytches and Brian Skinner, *New Wine-skins* (Eagle, 1991) Appendix D.

Chapter 13

1. The one known example is arguably an extended village anyway, but we have followed the incumbent's description.
2. *Going with God – Together: the Report of the Priorities for the Diocese Consultation 1988–89*, p. 70.
3. D Wasdell, Urban Church Work Papers, Nos 1 & 2.
4. Peter W Brierley (ed.), *Prospects for the Nineties: All England* (MARC Europe, 1991) p. 39.

Chapter 14

1. Robin Gill, 'More Pews than Parishioners', *Church Times*, 4 May 1990.

Chapter 15

1. See Appendix B for details of some of these.
2. See Charlie Cleverly's excellent book *Church Planting – Our Future Hope* (Scripture Union, 1991) for a fuller treatment.
3. Information in this section is drawn from Bruce Patrick, *The Life Cycle of the Reproducing Church* (New Zealand Baptist Home Mission Board, 1990).

Chapter 16

1. For an examination of these models see Neil Weston (ed.), *Taking on Faith in the Countryside* (Grove Books, 1991).
2. See my Grove Booklet, *Strategies for Rural Evangelism*,

(Evangelism Series No 5, 1989) for a more detailed reference to these types.

3. *Faith in the Countryside* (Church House, 1990), Ch. 11, Sec. 12, p. 246.
4. See John 5:19–20 and 2 Corinthians 6:1.
5. Chapter 4.

Chapter 17

1. See also G. W. O. Addleshaw, *The Beginnings of the Parochial System* and *The Development of the Parochial System* (both published by the Ecclesiological Society, 1986).
2. See Frank Barlow, *The English Church 1066–1154*, (Longman, 1979) pp. 51–52.
3. Peter Holt, *Moving Forward: A Strategy for the Diocese of Norwich* (1989), p. 12.
4. Stuart Blanch, *Future Patterns of Episcopacy* (Latimer House, 1991), p. 38.
5. Peter W. Brierley, *Christian England* (MARC Europe, 1991).
6. Foreword to David Pytches and Brian Skinner, *New Wineskins* (Eagle, 1991).
7. Ibid., pp. 38–41.
8. See the entry 'Lambeth Quadrilateral' in *Oxford Dictionary of the Christian Church* ed. Cross and Livingstone (Oxford University Press, 2nd rev. edn 1974).

Appendix A

1. C Peter Wagner, *The Four 'Rights' of DAWN*, International DAWN Report No 8, December 1989 p. 7.

New Wineskins

Bishops David Pytches and Brian Skinner

Defining new structures for worship and growth beyond existing parish boundaries.

With a foreword by John Tiller, Canon, Hereford Catahedral

The rigidity of the Anglican parish system, argue the authors, is a major hindrance for the church as it prepares to launch the Decade of Evangelism. The mobility of urban and suburban populations, coupled with the ever increasing variety of styles of worship and churchmanship already make a nonsense of the principle of worshipping within the parish one lives in. Yet the principle is sound.

Church planting should be part of the agenda, which means working outside the existing parish system. In this book Bishops *David Pytches* and *Brian Skinner* provide cogent arguments for breaking free from the existing boundaries and frustrations, and for relying increasingly upon the lay ministry, thus changing the role of the clergy. Their arguments are backed up with many examples where this has already been happening within the Anglican communion. Five appendices take matters into greater depth. *Stephen Abbott* on the fellowship of Christ the King, *Charlie Cleverley* on church planting, *Ian Bunting* on church growth in the north-east, *Bob Hopkins* on missions and church planting and *David Huggett* on frustrations within the current parish organisation.